Crazy Old Coot

A Curmudgeon's Stories about Bird Hunting and Life in the North Country

Jerry Johnson

Crazy Old Coot
*A Curmudgeon's Stories about Bird Hunting
and Life in the North Country*

Copyright 2014 by Jerrold L. Johnson

All rights reserved.
No part of this book may be reproduced without the written permission of Jerrold L. Johnson.

Cover design by Aaron Lurth

ISBN-13: 978-1500923242
ISBN-10: 1500923249

This book is dedicated to
Dave Wade
1943 - 2014
Great hunter, teacher, coach,
mentor and friend

Crazy Old Coot - A Curmudgeon's Stories

Also by Jerry Johnson

Hunting Birds
The Lives and Legends of the Pine County Rod, Gun, Dog, and Social Club

Scrawny Dog, Hungry Cat, and Fat Rat
A Tragedy for Children

Dispatches from a Northern Town
(blog on wordpress.com)

Contents

Introduction	Page	7
1. If I had a hammer	Page	11
2. Annie – Too much dog	Page	15
3. The hunting marketplace	Page	19
4. De Bat (Fly in Me Face)	Page	22
5. Crazy old coot	Page	26
6. Newton's Third Law	Page	31
7. Awe and wonder	Page	35
8. Lefever Nitro Special	Page	37
9. Hiraeth	Page	41
10. Badgering	Page	44
11. Just for the hull of it	Page	48
12. Zapping Pete	Page	52
13. Bells and whistles	Page	56
14. Project rifles	Page	59
15. Snowshoes of white ash and rawhide	Page	63
16. The 12 gauge .45-70 rifle	Page	67
17. The Eight Commandments	Page	70
18. Rabbitat	Page	73
19. Shoulder to the wheel	Page	76
20. Good decisions	Page	79
21. Squck	Page	84
22. One good dog	Page	87
23. Red elm	Page	91

24. Clay target games	Page	94
25. Punker spaniels	Page	99
26. The Charge of the Light Brigade	Page	102
27. Graceful double guns	Page	106
28. Red in tooth and claw	Page	109
29. North Country skunks	Page	112
30. Six-pocket pants	Page	116
31. Plinking	Page	119
32. If a bird fall…	Page	123
33. Fathers and sons	Page	126
34. Gus the enforcer	Page	130
35. Random advice	Page	134
36. Bird dog art	Page	138
37. Heaven's roads are gravel and sand	Page	141
38. Gone on ahead	Page	146

Introduction

"I am, beyond a doubt, the last of the old-timers."
    - Jack Crabb, from the movie Little Big Man, *based on the novel by Thomas Berger (1924-2014)*

Last of the old timers

BIRD HUNTING isn't what it used to be. But then, it never was.

Except in the stories of the old timers. The curmudgeons.

Of course the true reason for our abiding belief the world was better forty years ago is that we old timers were better forty years ago. Life can be hard, the decades of toil and tears have worn us down and worn us out, and we are not the men we used to be. But again, as I say, we never were. Except in our stories.

I did not ever intend to become an old timer or a curmudgeon, and I certainly never tagged myself with those labels.

The first time someone called me an older timer I resented it. He may have been stating a simple truth based on objective observation, maybe even complimenting me, but I didn't appreciate his candor and told him so. I crossed paths with this stranger a few years ago while we were both hunting the edges of a huge cattail marsh on a state-owned wildlife area. He was about twenty or twenty-five years of age and had a fat Labrador retriever and an automatic 12-gauge shotgun.

He admired my dogs and my gun. I was tactful and did not mention his. He told me pointing dogs were not the best choice for hunting pheasants in cattail sloughs. I mentioned that I had two birds in my vest and he had none. Then he said the fateful words:

"You know, old timer, I think you're the oldest pheasant hunter I've ever met."

Old timer?

"Listen, sonny," I said, "I'm not that old, and I'll still be hunting birds when you have given it up for golf. Or maybe knitting."

We went our separate ways without another word. Although it almost killed me, I refused to quit hunting the rough and marshy ground of that slough until I bagged my third rooster. The next day I lay on the living room couch, reading Hemingway's *Green Hills of Africa*, drinking beer, and taking ibuprofen and potassium pills as needed to calm the muscle spasms in my back and legs. Old timer! Humpf!

I told this story to one of my co-workers a few weeks later and she said, "My, you've become quite the curmudgeon." So there it was. In what seemed to be the blink of an eye I had gone from age thirty to sixty, a certified old timer and a curmudgeon, and I had acquired all the grumpy old man baggage along the way.

Now that I have reached that "certain age" in life, I understand and accept the wisdom of a proverb attributed to tribal elders of the Australian Aborigines: "In the end, the only thing you really own is your story." My story is all entwined with game birds, bird dogs, and bird guns. Maybe I own the story, but most days I think the story owns me. I've been at it so long I can no longer separate the singer from the song.

All of us old timer curmudgeons enjoy telling our stories, so frequently and in such detail that we drive family and friends to distraction – or worse, to glassy-eyed boredom. Called up from the vaults of memory, the stories do not always adhere to the actual facts and figures of historic events, but little matter. A story gets better with each telling as we take it out of the file, handle it and polish it a bit, show it off to admiring people, and then put the prettier and shinier version of the tale back into the vault for the next time.

One day, for no good reason I can remember, I decided to write some of those stories – the pretty and shiny versions, of course. A few dozen are published in this collection. There may be more in the making; I'm still hunting birds and started training a puppy last year. If all I will own is my story when my days are over and done, I want it to have an exciting final chapter and a really good ending.

Jerry Johnson, August 2014

Crazy Old Coot

Cherish the moments of awe and wonder in your life.
- Clement Seagrave

1

Be ready, and if'n a bird flies in front of you, just poke yer barrel at it and pull the trigger. That gun probly feels pretty big, but don't worry. She don't kick. Much.

- Advice from a well-meaning cousin to a ten-year-old boy on his first pheasant hunt

If I had a hammer

IF YOU WERE A BOY growing up in the rural Midwest in the 1950s you remember single-shot shotguns. That was the gun we all carried on our first hunts for pheasants, quail, grouse – whatever gamebird you dreamed about in your part of the country.

Made by Winchester, Harrington & Richardson, Stevens, Savage, Mossberg and several other firearms manufacturers for more than a century, break-action, exposed-hammer, single-shot shotguns were sold at local hardware stores in every small town. The receivers of many were stamped with the names of companies that were supposedly reputable "gunmakers" – Eastern Arms Company, Western Field, Springfield – which were really only gun distributors. Some even bore the name of the hardware store: Western Auto Store's Revelation brand guns, for example.

The single-shot handed to me for that first euphoric pheasant hunt on which I was permitted to carry a gun was a 12 gauge with a 30-inch full-choke barrel. The buttstock was cut down to fit a boy, it had a drop at heel of about three inches, and a rock-hard red rubber recoil pad was crudely attached. The hammer spring was so stiff that I could barely cock it back with one thumb, and the trigger pull was about as hard as clipping barbed wire with a dull wire cutter. The gun weighed more than seven pounds, which was a load for a small boy to carry on a cold morning's march through a muddy cornfield.

That break-action gun was functional, inexpensive, and ugly as sin, and with the possible exception of a best-quality Purdey sidelock gun I handled at a custom gunmaker's shop forty years later, it was the most exquisite firearm I have ever held in my hands. There was no doubt in my mind as I headed out on that first hunt with a gun that I would wield it with a natural grace and talent, kill at least three rooster pheasants stone dead in the air, and win praise and fame across the county.

The men who took us hunting in our youth never expected, I believe, that we would shoot a bird on the wing. If we had a chance to take a sitting cottontail or a squirrel on a tree branch we were encouraged to fire away – with supervision. But when a bird flushed, the chance for a shot was long past before we could cock that damnable hammer, shoulder the gun, and swing the heavy barrel in the general direction of departing tail feathers.

My bird hunter's garb was a pair of hand-me-down blue jeans with rolled-up cuffs and patches on the knees, and an oversized, oil stained denim jacket with the elbows in rags. A mother or aunt who apparently believed I was going on an Arctic expedition made sure I dressed in long underwear, a flannel shirt, and a heavy wool sweater before they stuffed me into the denim outerwear. Clad in knobby wool socks, canvas shoes and five-buckle rubber boots, I waddled out the back door like a drunken penguin.

I thought this was about as close to heaven as I would get in mortal life.

The opening day hunting party included my older brother, our cousin, three or four grown men, and an ill-tempered cocker spaniel-mix bird dog. Pure black and deviously misnamed Fuzzy, he preferred to catch and kill possums but would flush a pheasant under duress. If a bird tumbled to earth I would race madly after it, and if I beat the dog to it he would snarl and nip me. If he won the retrieving race, he would rip the bird into two or more pieces in the ensuing struggle for possession. At the time, I thought this was standard behavior for a bird dog.

Everyone hunted with a 12 gauge back then because anything less would have been "not enough gun," the mindset of the men who had come out of World War II with a healthy respect for heavy artillery. We were strictly cautioned to shoot only when it was "a sure thing," not so much for safety's sake as for conservation of ammunition. The price of 12 gauge shotshells had skyrocketed to almost eleven and one-half cents apiece, my father told me as he gravely handed me two shells to put in my pocket, and my cousin was given a stern rebuke for firing five rounds the previous season – almost sixty cents worth – without hitting even a rabbit. Sport was one thing, but these were the days when hunting also had to be justified as a cheap way of putting meat on the table.

The hunt itself was a long plod in a light rain through recently harvested cornfields, the barren stalks still standing higher than my head in those years of small farms when the tractor-mounted two-row corn pickers had not yet been superseded by the monstrous combines that chop the stalks at ground level. Weeds were thick between rows; this was before farm operators became chemically addicted and the land was still a living thing, not today's sterile and poisoned soil that functions only as a medium for growing the monoculture crop of corn or soybeans.

Despite my best efforts to keep pace with the men I was constantly falling behind and sometimes falling *on* my behind in the greasy, slippery mud. They would stop every so often and chide me to catch up. As I came straggling up at the end of one field, hot and sweaty and sulky, gun over my shoulder, I was kicking every clump and tangle in my path in a little fit of temper. One clump kicked back, and out of it came the Hindenburg dirigible, on fire, crowing and squawking, a huge rooster pheasant, flames shooting from his eyes and a trail of red smoke pouring from his tail.

My reaction was equal parts astonishment, terror, and panic. I finally regained enough composure to get the gun off my shoulder, cock the hammer, and fire a one-gun salute at the bird, now fifty yards distant and flying at Mach 1 speed. The shot did him no damage and probably caused him little fear or anxiety.

Shaking and humiliated, I opened the gun and examined the expended shotshell, warm and smoking and obviously defective. I looked up to see six faces staring at me with expressions ranging from distain to sympathy. "I think I knocked some feathers off him," I said in the most nonchalant voice I could muster.

"It looked to me like you did," my father agreed complicity. He took out his pipe and suggested that all the men have a smoke before continuing the morning's hunt. After a couple puffs he cautioned me, "Be a little quicker next time, because you've got just one last shell."

As the men smoked and talked my cousin sidled over with some consoling words. "Well, there was your first shot at a pheasant," he said, "and they don't get no easier than that, and you ain't got nothin' to show for it!"

He was not totally correct. True, I did not have a dead pheasant in hand, but I did have a bruised bicep muscle where the gun butt had kicked back when I pulled the trigger, a red spot on my cheek bone where the comb of the stock had hit me in the face, a bloody nose from the recoil-powered punch delivered by the thumb of my grip hand, and most important a tale to tell all the boys in school of how I had come "this close" to bagging my first rooster pheasant.

I also had my first dose of that addictive drug known as bird hunting, and knew I wanted more of it, as often as possible, every chance I could get. I vowed that someday I would have a fine shotgun, a peerless bird dog, a waxed-canvas shooting vest, and yes by god a pair of leather boots and a pipe. Most off all, there would be wonderful stories to tell every year about this best-of-life adventure.

It did not work out exactly that way, but my ten-year-old's plan to be a bird hunter came a lot closer to the mark than that first shot at a rooster pheasant. The excitement and anticipation of opening day returns each season, and the stories filed away in the vault of my memory will fill my daydreams until they haul me off to the bone yard.

That single-shot 12 gauge gun? It hangs on pegs over the door of my workshop where I can reach up and touch it as I begin each hunting trip. I'm not sure it brings me good luck, but it reminds me how lucky I have been for more than fifty years.

2

After twenty-five years experience raising, training and hunting English springer spaniels, I had the misguided belief that every dog had innate desire to bond with its owner, to become a loyal and affectionate partner, to work together as a team in the field, and to reminisce as a companion before the hearth. It took Annie, great teacher-by-example that she was, less than a year to disabuse me of that fallacy.

Annie – too much dog

ANNIE LOVED TO HUNT BIRDS. She just didn't like to hunt birds with me. If I were to admit an even harsher truth, I would say that Annie did not like me all that much and was tolerant of me only when we were afield in the fall and I had bird gun in hand.

Annie was a German shorthaired pointer, and she was possessed of all the irascible, obdurate, and contrary behaviors that characterize her breed. Plus the willful and defiant attitude specific to her personality. She rocked my confidence as a bird dog trainer and amateur canine psychologist. Over the course of eleven bird seasons, before I retired her, I recall eight or maybe nine great days of hunting together. Not a good percentage of our hundred or so ventures afield.

We were a dysfunctional pair. Actually, it may be stretching a point to say that we were a "pair" in the conventional meaning of the word. Our relationship was more on the order of work-release prisoner and parole officer. Like many a brilliant but sociopathic criminal, she thought rules and discipline were for chumps and marks. Released from heel, she would escape on a felonious rampage, heeding no call or whistle. Back in the travel box or kennel, she would look out on the world with golden, expressionless, insane eyes, unrepentantly awaiting the next breakout.

The confrontations and battles with Annie were of my own unwitting creation, of course. She was my first pointing breed bird dog. After twenty-five years experience raising, training and hunting English springer spaniels, I had the misguided belief that every dog had innate desire to bond with its owner, become a loyal and affectionate partner, work together as a team in the field, and reminisce as a companion before the hearth. It took Annie, great teacher-by-example that she was, less than a year to disabuse me of that fallacy.

Annie came from impeccable breeding. Unfortunately for me, that breeding was rooted in the genetic conversion of the once stolid, close-working German shorthaired pointer into a field trials racehorse. Hats off to the breeders who have mutated the GSP into a high-powered English pointer in both body conformation and psychotic hunting desire, if that is what they wanted, but what I wanted was a pointing dog more disciplined than demonic, more manageable than manic. I hunt birds on foot. A horseback hunter, or perhaps two or three of them, could have kept pace with Annie, but only an Olympic marathoner could hope to match her afoot, and even he could not do it running through heavy cover, encumbered by boots, vest, and a seven-pound shotgun.

To complicate the equation, I did not take possession of Annie until she was almost fourteen weeks old. This violated my cherished "forty-ninth day" early training principle, but in my ignorance and arrogance I was confident that we would bond. I was wrong. Annie, until the last six months of her life, never exhibited one flash of desire for human affection, or even human companionship. She was a bird-hunting machine – a wide-ranging, hard-running machine – and anything that was not part of the bird-hunting world was simply beneath her dignity and beyond her understanding.

Good days: Hunting the shortgrass prairies of the Dakotas, she was a thing of beauty and efficiency. I could see her out there, two hundred yards, three hundred yards, sometimes farther, coursing through the grasslands seeking sharptail grouse, prairie chickens, and Hungarian partridge. She would whirl around at first scent, lock into a classic point, one foot raised and the other three planted, as they say, on the coals of hell.

She would hold solid while I jogged the long distance between us. If I felled a bird, she would release from point the second it hit the ground, mark it down, and be on it with an intensity that would please a Labrador retriever trainer. She savagely bit each bird a time or two so that, in the event the bird was autopsied, it would be apparent that she, not I, had killed it. Early on she did not deliver a bird to hand but sort of threw it at me as she ran by so that she did not have to interrupt her return to the hunt.

After a year of force-training to retrieve and hold, she would grab the downed bird, stalk up to me stiff-legged, squat in a semi-sitting position, and we would engage in a brief tug-o-war before she would surrender possession. Then she was immediately racing off to the horizon, casting out so far there was the possibility that Canadian border security guards would be scanning the owner's information etched on her collar and calling my cell phone number to order me in to answer for numerous violations of international boundaries.

Bad days: All other bird hunts in aspen forests, Conservation Reserve Program fields, bean fields, brushy draws, and any other cover that required a bird dog that hunts less than a hundred yards away. I took her duck hunting one time. One time.

A hunting buddy once said of Annie, "That dog is a world class athlete!" True, but having a world class athlete on your team in the old men's softball league does not add to the enjoyment of the season.

When Annie was four years old, I threw in the towel, admitted my failure, and acquired a French spaniel puppy: Sasha. After that, Annie accompanied me on every bird hunting trip to the Dakotas and Nebraska. Sasha was my dog for all other hunts.

As she approached her thirteenth year, Annie was still in incredible physical condition. On our early morning walks around the perimeter of my hayfields I walk a little over a mile; Annie ran at least seven or eight miles. Just a warm-up. There were mornings we set out and I did not see her until a half-hour after I had returned. We were both okay with that. She would lie on the deck the rest of the day, waiting, waiting, waiting for the trip to Dakota.

When age finally caught up with her, the end came unbelievably quickly. One July morning, she jogged the morning workout route. In August, she walked it at heel beside me. In September, she walked to the hayfield gate, looked over the waving grass, and turned back home. A week later she could not get up without help, and the vacant and utterly confused look on her gray face told us it was time.

If there is a heaven for bird dogs, Annie's part of it looks just like the Fort Pierre National Grasslands, and she is running without limits. If someone is blowing a whistle to call her in, she is not paying any attention.

3

One does not hunt in order to kill; on the contrary, one kills in order to have hunted... If one were to present the sportsman with the death of the animal as a gift he would refuse it. What he is after is having to win it... through his own effort and skill...
   - from Meditations on Hunting *by Jose Ortega y Gasset (1883-1955)*

The hunting marketplace

IT WOULD BE BETTER for all concerned if I would stop hanging around sporting good stores.

Loitering is all I'm doing, since I have reached that time of life when I am no longer acquiring clothing or equipment for hunting, fishing or camping. Although I would probably buy a box of .22 rimfire cartridges once in a while if the flaky ammo hoarders weren't buying it all up in preparation for Armageddon or the invasion of the communist lemmings or whatever looming apocalyptic event fuels their paranoia.

But it is both informative and entertaining to hover around the fringes of the scene at Gander Mountain, Bass Pro Shop, Cabela's, Sportsmen's Warehouse, and similar "big box" sporting goods emporiums. Unobtrusively, I watch the current generation of outdoorsmen and marvel at the things they purchase and the curious things they say. The recurring message I hear is that hunting as we have known it is coming rapidly to an end, both in practice and in spirit.

Years ago I observed the typical, city-dwelling hunter's penchant for buying mechanical and electrical devices in lieu of investing the time necessary to acquire the lore of the hunt. Purchasing a predator call that is a battery-powered sound system with speakers and a remote control, for example, rather than learning how to use a simple mouth call has long been accepted in this practice of substituting money for learning. While I will not venture onto the slippery slope of what hunting equipment is ethical, this ever-increasing trend to replace painstakingly learned outdoor sports skills with easily acquired technology diminishes my respect for the "hunters" of this new age.

A strange logic has evolved with this culture of mechanized, computerized hunting. I hear comments that suggest the people who employ this stuff believe that it is somehow an integral part of the workings of the natural world. "I'm a predator," I heard one magnum-ammo buyer say last fall. "What predator wouldn't use every advantage he could get? If a wolf could get longer fangs, or a hawk could have sharper talons, they would use them."

Curmudgeon that I am, I was unable to refrain from tactfully commenting, "You're no predator!" Okay, to be honest, I did say, "Bullshit! You're no predator."

While he was still in shocked silence from being scolded by a crazy old man, I tried to shine a ray of light into his brain, which was apparently addled by watching too many of the so-called hunting programs on television. "A predator depends on his hunting skill for survival," I lectured. "If he fails to kill, he starves. If you fail, you go to the restaurant and order a hamburger."

I doubt he understood. After all, the point is to go out there and kill as many game animals as the law allows, as quickly as possible. Right?

Wrong. If that is your purpose, why not scatter some poisoned grain and kill them all? That would make you a first-class predator.

The central ethic of sport hunting is that we intentionally put limits on how we pursue and take game. We hunt only during a certain time of the year, within designated hours, on designated grounds. We accept limits on the number of game animals we will kill, the weapons and equipment we will use, the methods we will employ. We do not pursue them in ways that violate the concept of fair chase.

Unfortunately, since so much of today's hunting is done on game farms and preserves, with pay-by-the-bird "hunters" shooting pen-raised and semi-domesticated fowl, we may be losing all comprehension of the relationship between the hunter and wild animal populations and habitats. There is not much skill required, and not much sport involved, to shoot pheasants or quail that have no survival instinct or conditioning.

As a sad consequence, the hunt has become a stylized target shoot. You pay $25 per bird, the birds are released on the restricted grounds, and you shoot them. Sports as commercial recreation, merchandising and marketing.

All good business for the hunting preserve operators, the manufacturers and marketers of hunting clothes, boots, equipment, guns, ammunition, vehicles and paraphernalia. Good for tourism revenue for motels, restaurants, bars, and convenience stores. And the techno-hunters have a great time. Everybody wins.

Except the grumps like me who want the hunt to be the way it used to be. Change may be inevitable, but we don't have to like it.

So watch out for us when you buy your next piece of techno-gear at the sporting goods shop. You may be excited about buying that in-line muzzle-loader rifle with 3-9x40mm variable power scope and conical sabot slugs that make it the equivalent of a .30-06. But keep it to yourself. We don't consider that a primitive weapon and we're likely to tell you what we think, in no uncertain terms.

4

De bat he rat got wings, all de children know dat,
What I want to know from de lord is how you get de wings on de cat.
They say de bat got radar and he can fly through fan,
But what I am afraid are is that he got another plan.
To fly in my face, oh-oh, fly in my face, oh yeah,
I hope de bat he don't come out and fly in me face tonight.
One thing I forgot to tell you about the human race,
Everybody get a little upset when a bat fly in they face.
  – from the song De Bat (Fly in Me Face) *by Carly Simon*

De Bat

BATS STRIKE TERROR in my heart. Few things in this world can frighten me like a bat on the wing in the bedroom in the dark of the night.

Because our home is a 130-year-old log house built on a limestone foundation, bats have interrupted my slumbers several times over the past thirty years. It is a moment that tests a man's courage and resolve. No man who hopes to retain an iota of self-respect can, at these times, pull the covers over his head and beg his wife to get up and kill the bat. No, it is a man's job. A brave man's job.

Naturalists love bats and extol the virtues of these magnificent winged mammals that eat their weight in mosquitoes every night of a hot and humid Midwest summer. They even recommend (are you ready?) building bat houses in the back yard to attract and shelter them. Put up nesting boxes for bats, just as we do for the bluebirds and the wrens we love. Whatever.

I have tried to develop this same admiration and affection for the local member of the order *chiroptera*, commonly called the little brown bat (*Myotis lucifugus*), but to no avail. For I have looked them full in the face, these bats, their tiny but vicious faces that combine all the snarling menace and hatred of the wolf and the baboon, and I know them for what they are: Satan's flying rats from hell.

Despite its diminutive-sounding name, the little brown bat, in flight, is not little. Fluttering around a dark or semi-dark room, the little brown bat has a wing span of about four feet, a body length of about two feet, and a weight of four to five pounds. The talons on both the feet and wings are at least three inches long and razor sharp. Bat fangs are four inches in length and serrated, and bat ears are fringed with quills like those of a porcupine, but hollow and filled with venom that can numb or even paralyze a human body in less than twenty seconds.

And the bite of every bat, as you are well aware, is laden with rabies, Lyme's disease, typhoid, malaria, West Nile disease, cholera, bird flu, bubonic plague, and probably cancer.

Despite these facts, there are a number of people who advocate using a broom to chase the bat out of the house rather than kill it. I have even heard the suggestion that one should turn off all the lights inside the house, turn on a porch light, and open the windows and doors so that the bat can find its way out. This advice strikes me as being on par with closing one's eyes before dashing across a busy highway.

No, once a bat has chosen to enter my domicile, he has chosen death. The instrument of his demise will be the tennis racquet. I strongly advise keeping a tennis racquet in an easily accessible corner of the bedroom where it can be taken in hand at the first scream. Bats seem to be adept at avoiding blows struck with a broom or a folded magazine, but despite their radar-guided, jinking flight they can be intercepted by the sweeping stroke of a tennis racquet. I recommend the backhand stroke, not because it is faster or more accurate but because its follow-through is less likely to smash ceiling light fixtures, lamps, decorative vases, and other household objects.

When the bat has been struck in flight, bounced off one or more walls, and come to a crumpled rest on the floor, hit it several more times with the rim of the racquet, firmly but not so hard as to dent the wood flooring. This is also the appropriate time to cease shouting and cursing.

Unaccountably, when a bat is killed it shrinks in size to a few ounces, and its deadly claws, fangs and quills disappear. For this reason, chiropterologists, who apparently never encounter little brown bats in attack mode, mano a mano, in enclosed spaces, grossly underestimate its size and ferocity.

A number of people have suggested that I overreact to the presence of a bat in my house. I myself feel that I display an admirable level of self-control, considering the sudden appearance of danger. Grave danger, not only to person but to pride. From my point of view, if I am to be awakened from a sound sleep at 2 a.m. and told one of two things:

- There is a large brown bear prowling around the kitchen
- There is a little brown bat flying around the kitchen

I would much prefer the intruder be a bear. Not that I would be pleased to have a bear wandering around the kitchen, you understand, but I would not be quite as ambivalent about confronting him.

Imagine the scenario. I flip on the kitchen light, and there is a bear standing in front of an opened refrigerator door, deciding which cartons and containers to devour first. He looks over his shoulder with an expression of confusion and irritation, perhaps even a bit of anger at being interrupted in the middle of his midnight snack.

At gunpoint, I order him out. He refuses in his petulant ursine manner by ripping the door off the refrigerator, smashing the island cabinet, splintering the kitchen table, tearing the doors off several cupboards, and making nasty comments about the fact that we have no dishwasher and neither the tableware nor the plates and cups are full matching sets. I let him have five rounds of one-ounce slugs from a 12 gauge pump shotgun to settle his hash, and he expires, albeit messily, spattering blood on the walls, floor and ceiling, and doing considerable additional damage to the room, including pulling down the ceiling fan.

When the neighbors arrive to investigate the cause of all the shouting and roaring and screaming and crashing and gunfire, they find me in my underwear, somewhat bruised and battered, standing over a deceased nine hundred pound bear, amidst the wreckage of what was once a kitchen. I will be, understandably, babbling incoherently in a post-traumatic daze. My rants will weave around a core theme of "death to this bear and all others of his kind who dare to invade my kitchen." Or what remains of it.

Now, image the same scenario, more or less, but with the central role played by a little brown bat. And the shotgun replaced by a tennis racquet. Surely you can see the comparative effect these two situations would have on my reputation in the township. A sample conversation:

Neighbor One: "Did I hear that Johnson went on a rampage Thursday night and did $6,000 worth of damage to his kitchen?" Neighbor Two: "Yes, but it happened while he was killing a bear that had gotten into his house. A bear! A big brown bear!" Neighbor One: "Well, anyone in his right mind could have done that."

Versus:

Neighbor One: "Did I hear that Johnson went on a rampage Thursday night and did $6,000 worth of damage to his kitchen?" Neighbor Two: "Yes, and it happened while he was killing a bat that had gotten into his house. A bat! A little brown bat!" Neighbor One: "Well, no one in his right mind would have done that."

True. But when a bat appears in my house, I am not in my right mind. Not at all.

So, post-bat-incident, what should I do first? Order replacement doors for the kitchen cabinets, or try to repair the ceiling fan?

5

Every one is as God made him, and often-times a good deal worse.
- from Don Quixote *by Miguel de Cervantes (1547-1616)*

Crazy Old Coot

LIFE'S LONG PARADE of years and the trials and tribulations of fifty-plus seasons of bird hunting have shaped me. I have become a man of great dignity and character, the epitome of acquired wisdom, balanced temperament, sound judgment, keen perception, singular intellect, insightful reason, common sense, good humor, grace, generosity, compassion, patience, and of course an exceptional understanding of the nature of men and dogs.

At least that is how I like to see myself at this stage of life. Admittedly, there may be a few odd behaviors, peculiarities and quirks in the mix, but nothing that would overshadow the essential nobility of my person.

So I was appalled to learn that one of my long-time hunting companions has begun to describe me as eccentric. This annoyed me greatly at first, but on reflection I realized there may be a grain of truth in his observation, and the wise course would be to accept it.

Eccentric, I decided, is not a trait I should deny but a quality to which I should aspire. Not to the level of Crazy Old Coot, certainly, but with the aim of acquiring a reputation for being a bit erratic.

A few experiences during the past bird season led me to believe I am making excellent progress toward my goal – and with very little effort. The first came in October when I emerged from Minnesota's Chengwatana State Forest at the end of a morning's woodcock hunt and met another hunter in the parking area. He was a pleasant enough fellow, but as we made small talk he kept looking askance at my dogs Sasha and Abbey.

"Those dogs of yours springer spaniels?" he asked.

"No, French spaniels," I said. "Not real common down here. Lots of them in Quebec."

"Brittany spaniels?" he asked. Yeah, sure, I wanted to say. Forty-five pound Brittany spaniels with long tails, long legs, and square heads. But I was tactful.

"No. French spaniels. They're a pointing spaniel, like a Brittany, but not related."

"Hmm," he said. He loaded his chunky Labrador into his pickup and drove away. I imagine he wanted to share his morning's curious experience with hunting buddies at the bar.

"Met some weird old guy in the woods today. Had a couple of Canadian pointer dogs. Double-barrel shotgun, too. Wearing gloves with no fingers. Crazy Old Coot."

That was the day I became truly aware of my potential for eccentricity and vowed to play it for all it is worth.

Appearance is ninety percent of the game, they say, and all of us past the age of sixty can easily assume the eccentric look. Most of us do so anyway, whether or not we make a conscious effort.

Our balding heads, for example. A few years ago, after trimming the dogs on a hot summer day, I experimented with running the Wahl pet clipper over my thinning hair. The result was better than I could have imagined. My head looks like one of those threadbare family heirloom teddy-bears that has been dragged around by three generations of toddlers.

I go three weeks between shearings, which allows little salt-and-pepper tufts to emerge at various places on my scalp. Combined with a snow-white beard, this adds a touch of peculiarity to my appearance that gets me much faster service from medical clinic receptionists and bank tellers.

Choose your own level of personal hygiene, but I will note that the world is more accepting of a clean and well-groomed eccentric old hunter than one who might be a homeless vagrant who has become lost on the woods. Shower often enough that you do not smell like a well-used saddle on a sweated-up horse.

As to your bird hunting attire, here are some suggestions that have helped me in the pursuit of eccentricity.

Hat: A fedora-style felt hat is a good start, a style that is a blend of Fred Bear and Indiana Jones. Mine is a Stetson Three-River, I think, but it is twenty years old and so beat up and stained that I can no longer read the label. Some states require orange headgear for bird hunting, so you may have to wrap a couple turns of orange plastic marking tape around the hatband. Wonderfully eccentric.

Vest: Avoid vests from Orvis or Filson. Those are for wealthy, middle-aged, weekend hunters who are doctors and lawyers and accountants. Wear a strap vest, which can be worn over top of any number of layers of shirts without restricting your shooting motion. It has the added advantage of revealing rather than concealing the rest of your odd attire, and it has enough pockets, loops, clips and pouches to hold all the curious gear you'll want to pack along.

Compass: From your vest loops hang one aluminum-cased Engineers-style compass and one plastic Silva-style map-reader compass. One of the floating globe compasses that pin onto the shoulder strap of your vest is a nice touch, too. Never, ever carry a GPS unit.

Boots: Brown leather, not camo. Six-inch boots are good, eight-inch better. They must look battered, as if you have worn them through a few hundred miles of the roughest bird terrain. Use a one-inch dowel rod to beat the hell out of new ones until they look as though they have done at least five years of service.

Socks: Wool. Thick. Red. Put on a fresh pair each day; your feet smell bad enough already.

Gloves: Best if you wear no gloves at all, even if the temperature hovers near the zero mark, but if you must wear gloves, choose the rag wool fingerless type. As a concession to the dangers of frostbite at our age, you may wear a leather, insulated glove on your lead hand and the rag wool fingerless glove on your trigger hand. Allow your dogs to chew the wool gloves so they have the proper aroma.

Trousers: You can wear jeans, heavy wool trousers, light canvas work pants – chinos if you want – as long as you wear brush chaps over them. The chaps should be frayed, split, and ragged. If you buy new ones, get the dowel rod and some coarse steel wool and have at it.

Shirt: Bowing to hunting regulations, you must have some orange on your shirt, so take this nuisance to the limit and wear a shirt made entirely of that awful hunter orange cloth. When new, wash it six or seven times until it becomes faded and nappy and can easily pick up burs and seeds.

Gun: Although there is much to be said for the oddity of carrying a Browning Model 12 pump gun in 12 gauge with a 30-inch full-choke barrel, our goal is to be perceived as a wise and practiced Old Coot who may be crazy but has accumulated a wealth of hunting lore and skill. So you are going to have to shoot a few birds occasionally, and at our age we're not going to do that with an eight-pound cannon.

I recommend a side-by-side double, preferably a working man's American-made gun from the early 20th century because your gun must look weathered and worn and beaten, and not many of us are going to do that to a $20,000 English best-quality double. I advise 16 or 28 gauge guns for the obvious reason that 12 and 20 gauges are too conventional.

Dogs: You should choose a pointing breed, not a retrieving or flushing breed dog. Although an argument can be made for a ill-mannered Chesapeake Bay retriever or hyperactive springer spaniel if you let the dog ride in the cab of the pickup regardless of how muddy and you teach it to share your sandwich and drink from a thermos or beer bottle.

If you choose a pointing breed, it is perfectly fine to hunt over the traditional breeds – English setters and English pointers – if you have several of them. If you cannot put at least four setters or pointers on the ground, you must go with a more unusual breed. The German shorthair pointer, Brittany, Gordon setter, and even Vizsla have become so common that you will achieve, at best, fringe-eccentricity if you hunt over them.

I recommend a Weimaraner, Munsterlander, pudelpointer, Drahthaar, Griffon, or my personal choice a French spaniel. If the casual bird hunter cannot identify your dog, let alone pronounce its breed name, you are on the fast track to a solid reputation as a strange Old Coot.

Once you have acquired the look of an eccentric old hunter, add the characteristic speech pattern and cadence. In general, say as little as possible. Respond to questions with only a nod, which is second-nature anyway to those of us who have lost most of our hearing. If you must speak, limit yourself to simple words such as "Yah," or "Shoor," or "Mebbe."

When asked about your day of hunting, never mention numbers, such as "I got four grouse." Say "a few." All distances should be "a little ways" and all times should be "a while back." An entire summary of the morning's hunt, therefore, could be, "Yah, we got a few, a while back, just a little ways in, mebbe." In a lengthy conversation, it is good to subtly mention that you load your own shells, train your own dogs, do your own gunsmithing, and brew your own beer.

Describing the eccentric hunter's pickup truck is beyond the scope of this essay, but it should have a dented tailgate and a weathered topper. Have several old hand-made wooden boxes in the bed, each with sturdy hinges and latch. At least two should be secured by rusty padlocks.

Oh, and chew on a cigar. It never hurts to add a cigar for effect.

That should be all you need, and it's easy. Heck, I did it myself without even trying and seem to have struck the right balance. My hunting companions think I'm eccentric, but no one ever calls me a Crazy Old Coot. To my face.

6

For every action, there is an equal and opposite reaction.
  - Newton's Third Law of Motion

Newton's Third Law

ISAAC NEWTON was a physicist, not much devoted to the study of human behavior, but I find his Third Law of Motion to be more and more applicable to my social and political opposite reactions. To wit: Every time I encounter a "gun rights" action by the National Rifle Association, I react by moving farther into the "gun control" camp.

The most recent action-reaction incident was precipitated by a posting – a re-posting, actually – of an illustration that I believe came from the bowels of the NRA political lobbying division. To my dismay, this re-posting was by a former student of mine who had several gun safety and shooting lessons under my tutelage with the Luther College Shooting Sports Club a few years ago.

The illustration, at top, is a representation of a Ruger 10/22 semi-automatic hunting rifle in .22 Long Rifle caliber. A common and reliable rifle for small game hunting, this illustrated 10/22 was in "factory" configuration with a standard wooden stock, open sights, and a 10-round magazine. Immediately below it was an illustration of a Ruger 10/22 semi-automatic with numerous post-market devices to convert it to assault rifle appearance: pistol grip, folding butt stock, 50-round magazine, barrel shroud, laser sight, quick-release magazine lever – all in the familiar matte black color that has given the "black guns" segment of the arms industry its nickname.

The illustration has a caption: "It's the same gun!" It then goes on to say that in both squirrel rifle and assault rifle configurations this gun is exactly the same, so of course if there are any restrictions placed on ownership of assault rifles, why your old squirrel rifle will be illegal too!

This is a frequent and disingenuous claim of the NRA, people who allege to be small arms experts and yet insist there is no way to distinguish between, say, a Remington 1100 semi-automatic 12 gauge shotgun and an FAL semi-automatic 7.62mm military rifle. That is a blatant falsehood, but the NRA is not interested in accurate and honest discourse about responsible gun ownership and use, it is only interested in political lobbying and advocacy for firearms manufactures, who donate a lot of money to the NRA for these services.

(Actually, the NRA is interested in only one thing: the NRA. That is not my observation; it is that of Aaron Zelman, founder of Jews for the Preservation of Firearms Ownership, a zealous "gun rights" organization.)

For those naïve enough to accept the "it's the same gun" deceit, let me point out one significant difference (at least to me) between these two rifles:

If you come to my farm and ask to hunt, and you have a 10/22 squirrel rifle, you will be given permission to hunt.

If you come to my farm and ask to hunt, and you are carrying the assault rifle version of a 10/22, you will not be given permission to hunt. In fact, you will be immediately ordered to leave the property and not return.

That is because someone's choice of an assault-style rifle tells me something about his values and his character. I know immediately that this person is not a hunter, he is a shooter. Hunting is an honorable and noble venture that should be pursued with gear and guns that evidence knowledge of and respect for the sport's history, traditions and ethic. Black guns make a mockery of the essence and ethos of hunting. So, in my experience, do the owners of black guns, especially the one who, having failed to shoot a deer with his "home defense" shotgun, decided to use it to pulverize one of my wooden fence posts. Until that time, I was somewhat ambivalent about black gun owners. I offer him a hearty "well done!" for resolving my doubts. That equal-and-opposite-reaction law again.

I perceive that I am not alone in my dislike of black guns, weapons that have but one true purpose: to terrify and/or kill people.

Despite rambling and pernicious statements by "gun rights" advocates, these guns are not appropriate for hunting or target shooting. The sole function of a black gun is to kill people; "gun rights" advocates like to refer to this as "home defense" and "self-defense."

The tragedy for us hunters is that, thanks to the NRA, a growing majority of people are fearful of and opposed to all guns. Kudos to the black guns industry and its advocates, I suppose, for their success in convincing Americans that there is no real difference between a squirrel rifle and an assault rifle. The reaction they hoped for has gone astray, however. Their ludicrous promotion of assault rifles and handguns has not made people accept the legitimacy of ALL guns, it has made people oppose the legitimacy of ANY gun.

As a consequence, when hunters ask permission for access to land, we more frequently hear the response "We don't allow guns on our property." This is not much of an issue for me in my senior years. The misfortune is that my grandchildren will be denied this honorable and noble sport that has been important in my life.

Don't bother to express your concern about this to the NRA. If you investigate, you will learn the NRA does not give a bucket of cold spit about hunting. Or even about shooting, really. Check out the number of NRA-sponsored shooting ranges in your area. You can find none? No surprise.

The NRA is only interested in promoting the interests of gun manufacturers – the sale of guns. If you have a gun safe full of them, especially black guns, they have succeeded. If you have no place to hunt or shoot, that's not their problem.

Another thing that is not their problem? The increase in firearm homicides, virtually the only violent crime statistic that is going up every year. If you, like me, have a wife and son who teach in public schools, you live every day with the fear they and their students could be killed by someone who is an apostle of the black gun culture. Twenty-two first grade students murdered in five minutes with an assault rifle is small collateral damage, in the eyes of the "gun rights" advocates.

To convince me, a man who has owned and hunted with guns his entire adult life, to call for a ban on the sale of black guns, that reaction has required an incredible (and incredibly wrong-headed) series of actions by the NRA.

Congratulations, NRA! You have proved Mr. Newton's theorem.

7

And each one there
Has one thing they share:
They have sweated beneath the same sun,
Looked up in wonder at the same moon,
And wept when it was all done
For bein' done too soon,
For bein' done too soon.
For bein' done.
    - from the song Done Too Soon *by Neil Diamond*

Awe and wonder

CHERISH THE MOMENTS of awe and wonder in life.

Once upon a time, when we were young and strong and confident and immortal, we had the world and all the time in the world, dreams without limits and an unlimited number of new days and new wonders ahead. We were not foolish or insensitive, just ignorant and naïve.

Certainly we did not lack for daring, fervor, or passion. Then, perhaps even more than now, we were awed and enchanted by the rise of a full October moon over the rim of the shortgrass prairie, mesmerized by a night sky awash in stars, unpolluted by the glow of city lights. We were bright, shining, fiery, varied as the constellations, full as the Milky Way, endless as the Universe. We thought, if we thought at all, that we would witness these marvels, and these emotions, again and again, endlessly, thousands of moon rises, thousands of moments of splendor and excitement.

But on this autumn evening in the North Country, much later in life, the moon rise stirs passions more dulcet, mellow, bittersweet.

Most of our dreams have been realized, or have faded away like the last light of day, and those that we still hold are more modest and guarded. The years have not made us callous, exactly, but we are no longer naïve. We are too seldom excited to discover what life has to offer, and we are too often apprehensive to learn what life is taking away.

I do not mean to be overly maudlin. The joys of life are no less intense and gratifying in these years, but we savor them differently. Sunset, moon rise, storm at sea, dawn after an Arctic blizzard, the hug of a child, the kiss of a lover, an evening of talk with a long-time friend, the murmur and warmth of a fire in the woodstove. Through the passing years we learned these moments, these miracles of passion, are seldom and fleeting.

Do not take them lightly. Do not take them lightly. That full moon rising? You will stand in awe of it fifty times in your life at most, perhaps fewer. Perhaps many times fewer. A quiet night with someone you love in your arms and nothing else in the world of any importance? A hundred such nights? You would be among a fortunate few.

We have all sweated beneath the same sun. We have all looked up in wonder at the same moon. And we shall weep when it is all done, for being done too soon.

Cherish the moments of awe and wonder in your life.

Take you a workingman's lass and polish her bright as brass;
Dress her in such finery as she never hoped to see.
But in truth, oh how it hurts, you'll find 'neath silken skirts,
She's plain Judy O'Grady, not the colonel's fine lady.
  – Clement Seagrave

Lefever Nitro Special

WHEN WE FIRST MET and I picked her up in Reno, I could see that she had had some hard use. She had gone all gray and silver, and she was bruised and scarred here and there and most everywhere. A once shapely thing, now down on her luck and her looks.

But she opened up easily without squeak or rattle or sway, and a look down her bores showed she has no pitting or scoring inside, where it counted. She locked up tight with her action release lever still right of center, and her triggers both let off sharply and crisply with no bump or grind.

Her wood was solid and nicely grained, although the finish was gone and she had several scrapes, scratches, and nicks. Her butt plate was chipped and her checkering was worn smooth. Although the barrels were marked modified and full choke, I suspected they were tighter – probably full and extra-full.

I removed the forend, unlatched the barrels, held them up by the barrel hook, and tapped each with a fingernail. They chimed musically; nothing dull or flat about this lady's tune.

She was sixteen. Gauge. In years, she was probably eighty. I was smitten but was not ready to take her on as a reclamation project. I reassembled her, and as I was snapping the forend back into place I glanced at the serial number. Kismet. Its first four digits were the same as the final four digits of my Social Security number. Mon chéri, we were meant to be together.

She was a Lefever Nitro Special, a side-by-side double gun in 16 gauge. For $550 she was mine. Not an unreasonable price for tying the knot in Reno.

Back in the 1920s and 30s, the Nitro Special was one of a half dozen plain-Jane doubles that could best be described as a working man's gun. Similar, I suppose, to the ubiquitous Remington 870 pump action shotgun of today. Lefever double guns – the true Lefever guns designed and manufactured by D.M. "Dan" Lefever in the late nineteenth century – are truly fine guns, as good as or better than the Parker and L.C. Smith and A.H. Fox doubles that make aficionados of American classic guns swoon.

But the Nitro Special is a Lefever in name only, the brand name having been purchased by the Ithaca firearms company sometime after Dan Lefever died in 1906 and his namesake gun firm went belly up in 1919. The Ithaca-manufactured Lefever Nitro Special is a good, solid gun, but it is not in any sense a first-quality double gun.

Returning home to the North Country, I disassembled the Nitro Special and confirmed that it was mechanically sound. Matching the gun's serial number to the production dates for Ithaca-manufactured shotguns posted on the Internet, I learned it was made in 1928. That was good, because the 16 gauge guns manufactured that year all had 2 ¾-inch chambers, the standard length for today's 16 gauge shotshells, so I would not have to buy or load ammunition of 2 9/16 or 2 ½-inch case length.

I will not launch into a lengthy discussion, at least not here and now, of the relative philosophies and merits of restoration vs. modernization of an old double gun. Suffice to say, my goal was more modernization than restoration. To those who gasp and protest that modernization diminishes an old double gun's value, I remind that the gun's value was $550.

Double guns produced in the late nineteenth and early twentieth centuries have a number of characteristics and dimensions that differ from shotguns of today. Most have excessive drop at the stock's comb and heel, because shooting style and form was much different in that era.

They also have tight choke constrictions, necessary to shoot good patterns with the ammunition of that time. Other features that may trouble shooters include small trigger guards, pistol grips so close to the triggers that they cramp large hands, thick combs, short stocks, non-rebounding firing pins, steep forcing cones at the forward end of the chambers, and slightly over-size chambers. The wear and tear of years and usage also require repair: hammer springs, firing pins, hinge pin, extractors, wood finish, butt plate, checkering, engraving, barrel bluing, and receiver case-hardening – any or all of these may need attention.

All the repair and modernization work on this Lefever 16 was relatively simple. I removed the stock and had a friend who is a skilled woodworker cut it flat on top from comb to heel and then glue on a 1 ½-inch block of walnut that closely matched the old wood. I got to work with grinder, file and sandpaper and reshaped it to my exact dimensions, even including an almost imperceptible hollow at the comb where my cheekbone fits against the stock. The shallow pistol grip was not a problem, since my hands are small as those of the shotgunners a century ago.

Using a wet rag and heated metal bar, I raised some of the bruises and gouges, sanded out others, and left several that give the gun character. Ahlman's gun shop in Minnesota did the checkering on stock and forend to my specifications. I thought about an oil finish but opted for polyurethane varnish. From Brownell's in Iowa, I ordered a recoil pad that made the length of pull correct for me.

The necessary metal work was done by a competent gunsmith: chokes opened to improved cylinder and improved modified constriction, forcing cones lengthened, action parts cleaned and tested, trigger pulls lightened to 3 ½ (right barrel) and 4 pounds (left barrel). Bluing barrels and restoring case hardened colors to the receiver have become expensive. The gunsmith applied a less costly black-coat process to both the barrels and receiver. It has held up quite well over five years, and it looks even better after some weathering.

The whole modernization project, since I did much of the woodwork myself, cost less than $500. The market value of the gun may not be the $1,000 spent acquiring and modernizing it, but it is worth that much and more to me. It has taken pheasants, sharptail grouse, prairie chickens, woodcock, ruffed grouse and a few doves over the past five years.

Although I would like to say I shoot it better than any of my other double guns, that would not be true. But my misses are seldom the fault of the gun. Nor has this Lefever Nitro Special been transformed, Cinderella-like, into a top-quality double gun. She isn't a princess, but she's a damned good-looking and well-proportioned working girl. And they are more my type.

9

Hiraeth (n.) (Pronunciation: heer-ath) – A Welsh word that has no direct English translation; implies a longing or homesickness tinged with grief or sadness over the lost or departed, a yearning or nostalgia for a place or a home to which you cannot return, which may in fact never have truly existed.
   -Definition from North Country Dictionary *(unpublished)*

Hiraeth

OF THIRTY-SOME HUNTS in the shortgrass prairie country – Nebraska, South Dakota, North Dakota – the best were the ten or twelve trips when we camped. The days spent walking over native grassland preserves of 100,000 acres in pursuit of sharptail grouse, prairie chickens and Hungarian partridge were a bird hunter's paradise, but my most cherished recollections of those adventures are memories of times in camp.

I miss hunting camp. The logs burning slow in the fire ring, the meals cooked over a Coleman stove or open flames, the soft glow of autumn evenings, coyotes yelping out on the prairie, the magnificence of a night sky unpolluted by any trace of city lights, cool breezes rustling the last of the leaves on the cottonwood trees around the campsite, sleeping in tents, the too-warm sleeping bags, the snores of dogs and hunting companions, the breakfast coffee percolator bubbling at the fire's edge.

Six autumns we camped at a place called Beeds Landing on the east side of Merritt Reservoir, adjacent to the Samuel R. McKelvie National Forest near Valentine, Nebraska. There is no forest there, by the way. It is a grassland, established as a federal preserve by naming (misnaming?) it a "national forest."

Some years there were as many as seven of us in the hunting party, and one year only two. Big group or small, all were great campouts, and most were a good week of bird hunting in the McKelvie. I wish we could go back there this fall to spend a few evenings in friendship, drinking warm beer, smoking cigars, and warming our aging bones by the fire as we tell lies about hunts of the past.

Yes, I remember there were trips when our camp was buried under three inches of snow, tents blown down by forty mile-per-hour winds, equipment and clothing and food soaked by driving rain, water jugs with a half-inch of ice on top on frosty mornings, dog food bags raided by raccoons, and kitchen gear and cookware scattered by ground squirrels and blue jays. I often came home with blisters on my hands, an aching back from sleeping on the ground, jackets and pants speckled with holes burnt by embers blown from the fire, guns and gear coated with fine sand, and needle-spine sandburs clinging to everything.

But the good memories far outweigh the bad. It has been more than ten years since the last hunt from a camp, and sadly the last traces of wood smoke scent have faded from my favorite hunting coat. The shooting vests and hunting pants with grit in the folds and pockets were long ago worn out and discarded. One enduring token: every now and then I still find one of those damned sandburs hiding in an old glove or sock or sweater.

We, the Over the Hill Gang, still plan our annual shortgrass prairie bird hunt, and about every other year we actually go. But now that we are all in our sixties, motels and small-town cafes have become our natural habitat on hunting trips. I keep proposing one more hunt from tent camp, but I don't get any takers. Camp chores that used to take twenty minutes are now an hour's labor, and it is dispiriting to force arthritic, worn out body parts to function after a night in a sleeping bag in a tent.

Even if I have to go by myself some October, I'm camping one more time in the Nebraska Sandhills. It is a country that holds onto me and draws me back, a place of spiritual awakening, and I need to renew that every few years.

Like most folks who spend much time in the wilderness, there came a moment I wandered into an ethereal intersection of place, time and consciousness that spun me into a sort of existential vertigo. It was a moment that made me starkly and frighteningly aware that I was, paradoxically, physically insignificant in this universe but spiritually connected to everything. For some people this revelation is inspired by the vastness of the night sky, the colossal austerity of a mountain range, or the endless sweep of open sea, but for me it was the Sandhills.

Thereafter, each day of hiking the dunes and flats of that country was a revival of that spiritual awareness and the emotions that wrap around it. If it is possible to love a country, then I love the Nebraska Sandhills. I find sanctity there that I find in no other place, a sense of peace and wonder and excitement.

I wish I could say my Sandhills epiphany has lifted my character and ethos to a higher level, but that is not the case. However, it did let some of the hot air out of my inflated sense of self-importance, inspire me to live more in the moment and less in the past or future, and allow me to savor the simple joys of life more fully and dismiss the disappointments. In camp, those evenings by the campfire with a good beer and good cigar are all the better when your heart, mind and soul are at peace.

Although I do not talk much about this, lest friends think my senility is advancing apace, I want my ashes scattered in the Sandhills after my death in the hope that there is something infinite and universal to connect with. I trust there will be a few more days spent hiking and hunting those hills before that final visit.

Maybe this October.

10

The last word in ignorance is the man who says of an animal or plant, "What good is it?" If the land mechanism as a whole is good, then every part is good, whether we understand it or not. If the biota, in the course of aeons, has built something we like but do not understand, then who but a fool would discard seemingly useless parts? To keep every cog and wheel is the first precaution of intelligent tinkering.
    - from Round River: The Journals of Aldo Leopold, *by Aldo Leopold (1887-1948)*

Badgering

THE BADGER that lives on the edge of the big hayfield made it through this hard winter of 2013-14. Although I have not yet seen him in the flesh, I found evidence of his survival after the last traces of snow melted away: one of his excavations on the north edge of the field where he was burrowing for pocket gophers, a favorite entree.

Although the badger and I are not friends – far from it; he treats me like his most detested enemy whenever we meet – I was pleased to know that he is still living and apparently prospering in the rough woods and brush lands on the borders of the farm. He has chased me, growled at me and snapped at me with murderous intent, but the place would be something less without him, and I want him and his kindred to dwell here as long as I do.

While the other large mammals of the Great Plains – the grizzly bear, cougar, wolf, bison, elk – have been exterminated over the past 200 years, the badger has held on, albeit in limited numbers. Most zoologists attribute the badger's survival, and the extinction of his erstwhile mammalian peers of the prehistoric era of native grasslands, to suitable habitat. Scattered remnants of marginal land that can support badger populations still remain among the millions of acres of the plains that have been reduced to sterile, lifeless soil by the agricultural practices of our industrial society.

Also, the badger spends much of its life in subterranean haunts and was therefore less visible to the early white settlers and farmers who naturally saw all wildlife as a food source.

I disagree. Based on my own experiences with badgers, I contend that they are the perpetrators of the demise of the bear, wolf, cougar, elk, bison, and probably several dozen other late lamented species of wilderness wildlife. My theory is that the badgers, in a Darwinian maelstrom, slaughtered them by the millions, ate them nose to tail, and gloated over the carcasses, using splinters of their bones as toothpicks

Admittedly, my knowledge of the badger's predatory behavior is based on a few brief and highly active encounters when I was not disposed to pause for careful and considered observation, or to take detailed notes, photographs or video footage. In each instance I was running at 22 miles per hour (my animal encyclopedia says that a badger can run, in short bursts, at speeds up to 21 miles per hour) and was engaged in distractions that included shouting, leaping, whistling, waving and kicking at both the aggressive badger and my dogs. The dogs, being much faster and agile than I am, found these badger adventures highly entertaining and begged for repeat performances.

Yes, the American badger (*Taxidea taxus* of the taxonomic family *Mephitidae*, a not too distant relative of the skunk) is a nasty customer. They are squat-bodied, short-legged, thick, muscular, surprisingly large (up to 35 pounds), reclusive, ill-tempered, territorial, tenacious and aggressive when disturbed. Much like me in almost all particulars.

A badger is a digging machine with powerful forelegs and shoulders, long claws, and a passion for earth-moving that shames the most astute backhoe operator. Its focus on excavation is so intense that if you should come upon one that is madly tunneling in pursuit of a mole you can literally grab it by the tail before it becomes aware of your presence. I do not recommend this, however. For one thing, its tail is quite short and difficult to grasp; for another, the badger does not like having its tail grabbed and expresses this dislike in a most vehement way.

I discovered this seven or eight years ago when my bird dog Sasha seized a burrowing badger by the tail on warm evening in June. A Keystone Cops slapstick pursuit scene ensued.

The badger chased Sasha, snarling and clicking its teeth and snapping its broad, flat head back and forth to express its irritation. Fearing the badger would bite and maim my dog, I chased after them, blowing my training whistling, shouting, and threatening bodily harm to both. Not the least intimidated, the badger turned and chased me for ten or twenty yards with Sasha close behind barking and nipping. I would like to think Sasha was coming to my rescue, but in truth she was acting out of sheer enjoyment.

When she clipped the badger's rear with her teeth, it whirled around, threw itself onto the ground and thrashed wildly in a performance of rage and abuse that would have done credit to any World Cup soccer player dramatizing his faux injury to the cameras. But in ten seconds it was up and running for its den in the woods with Sasha in chase and me running behind. This turn-and-turn-about game of death tag continued for several more minutes until I caught hold of Sasha's collar and dragged her from the field of battle.

The badger made two short dashes after us, cursing in badger-ese that we were %$* cowards and @#&! scum and should stand and fight like warriors instead of prancing away like pink-dirndl-clad schoolgirls. Sasha was up for the brawl, but I declined. I'm the one who pays the vet bills, not her.

When I tell this story in hunting camp I insist the badger was a boar with huge fangs and gallons of mating-season testosterone coursing through his veins, but for all I know it was a sow with a den of cubs somewhere waiting for her to come home with a mole or gopher for dinner. I was grateful that they did not dine on *canis lupus familiaris* or *homo sapiens*. Badgers are omnivores, and we were omni.

A bit of badger lore: If you choose to hunt badgers on purpose, the dachshund was originally bred as a badger-hunting dog. The German word for badgers is *dachs*. The dachshunds I see these days do not appear to be practitioners of the sport.

More badger lore: They live in clans called cetes, a group of two to a dozen badgers. I do not know if the members of a cete are sworn to revenge the murder of a member of their clan, but I'm not taking any chances.

Badger lore from the publication *Animal Friends of the Southwest* by Fran Hubbard:

"Badgers can be fierce animals and will protect themselves and their young at all costs, are capable of fighting off dog-packs and fighting off much larger animals, such as wolves and bears."

Oh, really?

And…

"However, badgers can be tamed and then kept as pets."

Yeah, whatever.

I like them living on the marginal land on my farm. I really do. But we have agreed that they keep to their territory, I keep to mine, and a few passing encounters each year is enough for all of us.

11

Shotshell hulls of many different brands and configurations show up in the reload pile, but I use only Winchester AA hulls. This is a narrow, biased, personal prejudice. Forty-plus years of reloading has given me a terminal case of OFS (Old Fudd Syndrome), characterized by diminished ability to reason and increased irrational outbursts such as "I've always done it this way!"

Just for the hull of it

THE THERMOMETER on the deck reads twelve degrees below zero on this sunny but "brisk" March morning in the North Country. The farm is covered by thirty-some inches of accumulated snow as we near the end of winter, and an Arctic wind is gusting at twenty miles per hour as I venture out in shirtsleeves with the dogs, cup of hot coffee in hand, to grab a chunk of red elm firewood for the stove.

In short, this is a perfect day to retreat to the warmth of the workshop and fuss with the shotshell hulls waiting to be reloaded.

From April through September, time and weather permitting, I shoot a couple thousand rounds of shotshells at skeet, trap, sporting clays and five-stand ranges. Unlike my wiser friends who do all their clay target shooting with one gun, or at least one gauge, I usually shoot my field guns –double guns in 12, 16, 20 and 28 gauge. So on this winter day, as I enter the "reloading season," a multi-colored mountain of shotshell hulls in plastic bags lies piled on the floor in front of the reloading bench.

Empty shotshells are called "hulls," because... well, there must be some plausible explanation of how the word "hull" came to be applied to shotshells, probably derived from the definition of hull as "the hard shell or outer covering of a seed or fruit." And hull is much quicker and easier language for gun writers than "cylindrical, straight-walled, poly-composite tube attached to a circular, rimmed base of brass." So, "hull" it is.

Preparing hulls for reloading brings out my latent obsessive-compulsive tendencies. This madness takes hold with the first step in the process, sorting and culling a couple thousand hulls, first by gauge and then by brand and type. Dividing them into piles of 12, 16, 20 and 28 gauge is fast and easy; sorting them by type takes longer.

Hulls of many different brands and configurations show up in the reload pile, but I recognize only two categories: Winchester AA hulls and junk hulls. This is a narrow, biased, personal prejudice. Forty-plus years of reloading with Winchester AA hulls has given me a terminal case of OFS (Old Fudd Syndrome), characterized by diminished ability to reason and increased incidence of irrational outbursts such as "I've always done it this way!"

A less hidebound reloader would accept the truth that Federal produces excellent hulls, as do Remington, Fiocchi and Cheddite. But all my reloading machines are set up for Winchester AA hulls, so, dammit, that's the only brand I'm going to use! The exception is 16 gauge hulls. Since Winchester no longer produces them, I use Cheddite Multi-Hulls purchased from Ballistic Products Inc. in Minneapolis (http://www.ballisticproducts.com).

Now comes the more agonizing part of the process: eliminating the hulls that are damaged, worn, or otherwise unsuitable for another reloading. I fuss over the piles of battered hulls for an hour or more. Although I want to credit this mania to my being a meticulously safe and careful reloader, the truth is that I am just a tightwad. It pains me to throw away a 10-cent piece of plastic (14 cents if it's a 28 gauge hull!) that may be in good enough condition for one or two more reloadings. A cloth soaked in Armor All vinyl cleaner is always at hand to perform a sort of emergency CPR on hulls that show any spark of life. An ailing hull has to go to great lengths to prove to me it is no longer worthy of service.

Alas, despite my best revival efforts, about ten percent of the hulls will have to be discarded each season. Any that have a crack or split in the shaft will be immediately rejected, of course, but that is a rare occurrence.

A hull will also be weeded out if it has a black ring around the primer, evidence of an expanded primer pocket that could result in a gas blow-by that could injure the shooter's eye. A more likely danger is that a primer will slip out of a loose primer pocket at a "Murphy's Law" moment – during the feed-and-chamber cycle from the magazine of a semi-automatic gun. The escaped primer will wedge itself under the feed pawl and jam the whole works, forcing you to take the entire action apart to extract it.

Not that this has ever happened to me. At least not twice.

Now come the tough decisions: which hulls have become too weary to hold a tight crimp? Throw out any hull that has splits in the rim of its mouth, where repeated crimping and firing have cracked the plastic.

What about those hulls with rims that are intact but frayed, paper-thin, soft, or brittle? If the top edge is burned black and looks a bit ragged from multiple firings, it's easy to toss the hull.

The demons are the ones that still appear shiny and smooth and firm – with just one or two little creases or incipient splits. Those treacherous rogues will promise to seal tightly but will slowly open on a hot day, spilling their charge of shot to rattle around in the bottom of the ammo box. I prefer light target loads, but not "unintended" light loads.

One more step: lightly wipe each hull with that Armor All-soaked cloth to remove any grit or grime you do not want to introduce into the action or chamber of your shotgun. Do not get too finicky in this process; there are a couple thousand of these things to clean, and you have but one lifetime.

So, at last, you are done and can gaze down with satisfaction at a half dozen plastic bags full of hulls ready to be reloaded. While you were engaged in these hull preparation chores, your shooting buddies have car-pooled to the sporting goods store, each purchased four flats of bargain-priced shotshells, and are sitting around a tall table in a sports bar, drinking beer and watching a basketball game on a big screen television.

Take heart in the knowledge that the cheap "factory loads" they have purchased will be sadly inferior to the loads you will produce with these nicely prepped hulls. But I will have to expound on the art and science of shotshell reloading in a future essay. For now, I can't stand to look at another empty hull.

12

Everybody loved Pete, but he was not what you would call a reliable teammate. Sometimes he would win games for you with amazingly brilliant performances, and sometimes he would lose games for you with amazingly stupid performances.

Zapping Pete

PISTOL PETE was the most lovable and most frustrating bird dog of the dozen or more that I have trained and hunted over these past four decades. An English springer spaniel, he was the progeny of an outstanding field trials dog and possessed immense talent, strength, stamina and drive. But his potential was unfortunately hampered by his limited mental capacity.

We have all known a "Pete." He may have played defensive tackle on your high school football team, a position that did not require great mental acumen.

"Pete" did not have the analytic and interpretive skills to recognize the opposing team's offensive formations, or to read and react to the moves of the guard across the line of scrimmage. But he had incredible athletic ability, so he won his place in the starting line-up by single-mindedly carrying out the coach's instructions: Find the ball, and then go get it. Which he frequently did, in his own wild and undisciplined way, because he was big and strong and played with unbounded enthusiasm.

On Saturday night, "Pete" was the guy who came late to the unofficial "victory party" in the city park, a six-pack of beer hanging on his belt, a fat cigar jutting from his mouth, a white X of athletic tape holding his broken nose in place, and a huge smile on his face that told you he was happy just being there. Unintentionally and obliviously he would block the driveway with his car, knock the cassette player off the picnic table, sit in the pizza on the park bench, blow cigar smoke in your girlfriend's face, tell locker room jokes, belch and fart, holler "We kicked their ass!" and fall into the duck pond about the time the police drove by on night patrol in the hope of snaring some minors in illicit possession of alcohol.

Everybody loved "Pete," but he was not what you would call a reliable teammate. Sometimes he would win games for you with amazingly brilliant performances, and sometimes he would lose games for you with amazingly stupid performances. A physically gifted but intellectually deprived fellow with a happy-go-lucky zest for life, he was decidedly not the consummate team player. No one ever said, "Someday, Pete and I are going into business together." Not even furniture moving.

That was the character of Pistol Pete, my springer spaniel, in a nutshell. Short-legged, barrel-bodied, thickly muscled, broad-headed, he was huge for a springer, probably forty-five pounds. To this day I believe he was part Labrador retriever, a suspicion confirmed by his love of water, manic retrieving desire, body conformation, raven black markings, square head, thick tail, and especially his tendency to go brain dead the moment bird scent entered his nose.

If I had had the wisdom to train him and hunt him as a non-slip retriever, his autumn days spent only in the duck blind, he could have been a star. The defensive tackle hunkered down in four-point stance, waiting and watching as the gun is fired and the duck or goose falls, then exploding from the blind with frenzied purpose to find and catch and bring it to hand. That could have been Pete's forte.

But upland hunting, for a flushing breed dog, is more like playing free safety. You must recognize the formation, analyze and predict the action, read the keys, react to the ebb and flow of the play, instantly discern action from feint, fill the gap to stop the run, position yourself to intercept the flight of the pass, anticipate and outsmart your opponent ...

Pistol Pete was capable of none of this. "Find the ball, and then go get it." That was Pete.

He made three or four of the greatest retrieves I have ever witnessed, including one Herculean, thirty-minute, mile-long, run-

and-swim chase across a huge marsh wildlife area. Those great moments were offset, however, by the dozens of times he put to wing flocks of pheasants, coveys of quail, or pods of sharptail grouse, all a hundred yards or more distant from the gun while I violently screamed "HUP!" and blew blasts on the whistle that would drown out a calliope. Once bird scent entered Pete's olfactory nerve, he was impervious to all other stimuli.

My days with Pete were in the early era of the electronic training collar. A more nuanced training tool now, and one that I use carefully at times, that little black box with electrodes that press against the dog's neck allows the handler to press a button on a transmitter to administer an electric shock to the dog. The training collar I now own has fifteen levels of stimulation, ranging from a tingle that I can barely feel on the palm of my hand to a jolt that is quite painful.

But it was a much more primitive training collar that I borrowed twenty-five years ago to use as a last resort to stop Pete from bolting when he hit bird scent. The transmitter had one control button, and the level of stimulation was regulated by choosing one of three "chips" to insert into the black box: green, yellow, red. A tyro at using this thing, I inserted the green chip (lowest level) one November morning, strapped the collar on Pete, and took him pheasant hunting.

We found a clutch of hen pheasants on the edge of an unharvested cornfield, and they ran to escape. Pete chased after them, out of control, and after giving him fair warning with two whistle blasts I pressed the transmitter button. He showed no sign that he felt any shock from the collar and flushed the hens at the far end of the field a few hundred yards away. He came bounding back, as always, happy to have done so well.

I took off the collar, exchanged the green chip for the yellow chip, and fastened it back around Pete's neck. It was more than twenty minutes before we found another pheasant, this one a rooster that was a veteran of the hunt. He ran out of the bean field, ducked through the fence, and scuttled along the bottom of a roadside ditch with Pete in hot pursuit. I blew one blast on the whistle, Pete ignored it, and I punched the button. The results were dramatic.

Pete went airborne about five feet, he yelped in pain, his eyes bulged, his ears shot out horizontal from his head, he leaked a stream of pee, and I believe I saw a puff of steam shoot out his nose. He immediately ceased pursuit of the rooster and came staggering back to me. I checked the chip. Yes, it was yellow, the "medium" level of stimulation. My assumption was that the red "high" level chip must knock the dog unconscious, if it was a large breed, or kill it outright if it was a smaller breed. I chose not to try it.

That one lesson was all it took to train Pete. Thereafter, whenever I put the collar on him, he walked at heal and refused to hunt. When I took the collar off, he hunted with all his former enthusiasm, ignored the whistle as he always had, and flushed birds out of range with even greater abandon.

Except for doves and ducks, Pete seldom hunted with me after that. He had out-dumbed me, and I threw in the towel.

Pete is long gone, but I still keep a memento on the shelf to remind me of days spent afield with him: a small plastic football helmet with a bent whistle jammed into the face guard.

13

I like them all – pointers, setters, retrievers, spaniels – what have you. I've had good ones and bad of several kinds. Most of the bad ones were my fault and most of the good ones would have been good under any circumstances.
  - Gene Hill (1928-97), hunting and fishing writer

Bells and whistles

NEW PUPPIES come with bells and whistles. Literally. When each new puppy comes into our home, I celebrate the event by buying a new training whistle and a new collar bell.

It seems ridiculous, I know, to place this bell-and-whistle set in the box with a newly weaned puppy that is barely larger than the bell, but it has become a tradition. What I'm doing, symbolically, is making a promise to the pup that I will raise and train it to become the best bird dog it has the potential to be. I'm also making a promise to myself that I will open my heart and go through bird-dog-and-bird-hunter cycle of joy and sorrow one more time.

The same whistle and bell do not always accompany the dog through its entire lifetime, but often they do. And a few sets of bells and whistles were buried with their owners over the years when Zeke and Suzy and Pete went on to their rewards in that bird hunting heaven the spiritual part of me wants to believe in. Urns of ashes are the resting places for the souls of more recent dogs, so their bells on tattered collars and their whistles on stained and frayed lanyards hang on the clubhouse wall.

If I take down one of these whistle-and-bell sets in the quiet of the evening and handle them gently, bringing them to my nose in imitation of a bird dog's scent-information gathering, my mind is flooded with memories of times shared with Molly or Herco or

Annie... Good times, bad times, hard times, easy times, happy times, sad times, angry times, joyful times. All the experiences and emotions of a lifelong friendship with a beloved hunting companion.

Bells and whistles have it all over the fading photographs tucked into seldom-opened albums, photos which for some reason never show the dog as it really was, and reveal nothing of its character or personality. A dented brass bell or a plastic whistle with mouthpiece cracked from where I bit down on it hard in raging frustration – these present a much more accurate and vibrant picture, at least to me.

But we are talking about the joy of assigning new bells and whistles to seven-week-old puppies, the promise of days ahead, not the remembrances of days past.

My bell-and-whistle tradition is based in part on craft and mysticism, and in part on hope and sentiment. The craft and mysticism part has to do with the dark corner of my ego that refuses to admit that failings in bird dog training could be in any way my fault. Obviously, if I had the right whistle its tone would reach into the depths of the brain of the most obtuse and stubborn dog, turning on the light and opening the channels of communication so that it would understand and accept my every command, conform to my every instruction in the field, even anticipate my thoughts and whims.

Attention, devotion, obedience – all to be had by a pip on the whistle. If only I could find the right whistle.

I have tried at least a dozen makes and models: plastic, metal, horn, wood; high pitch, low pitch, blended pitch; loud, moderate, soft; even two types of silent whistles. Despite decades of dutiful and disciplined whistle-training lessons I have still not discovered "the one."

But I have not given up. The perfect whistle is out there, and hope springs eternal that I may someday discover it. (Reality knocks this theory down regularly when I realize that my dogs respond equally well to any of three or four different models of whistles, and perhaps listen ever better when I whistle through dirty fingers stuck into the corners of my mouth.)

The bell plays a similar function except that I, not the dog, am the one being sound-trained. As my hearing loss has steadily worsened, the bells attached to my dogs' collars have made a progression from jingling sleigh bells to ringing goat bells to clanging cow bells. I have now gone back to the smaller sheep bell size because I cannot hear any bell, regardless of tone. The bell is for cosmetic reasons only, although I think the dogs like it because it is an icon of the hunt and a good excuse to tell me, "Hey, if you can't hear the bell and keep track of me, it's your own damn fault!"

Some of my hunting cronies have wisely decided to equip their dogs with GPS locator collars, but I rationalize that my dogs hunt pretty close and I always know where they are. And I'm convinced the ringing of the old-fashioned brass bell triggers some set of synapses in the dog's brain that remind it to hunt to my range and check back every few minutes. Usually.

Hope and sentiment are the other motivations for the bell-and-whistle tradition. It's like placing a softball in your granddaughter's cradle, I suppose, or a baseball in your grandson's. You're not expecting them to become professional players some day, but you want to pass on your passion for the game and hope they love it, too.

A special bell-and-whistle set hangs near the container that holds the ashes of my tough-minded, strong-bodied English springer spaniel, Herco. He's waiting for me to join him so that we can be scattered together in the Nebraska Sandhills. Maybe someone will honor our passing with one last blast on the whistle and one last ring of the bell. I'd like that.

Was he my best-ever dog? I don't know. All of them were good, and I liked them all. But in our rough, masculine way Herco and I knew each other and loved each other better than any of the rest of my canine partners. If there is a happy hunting ground waiting on the other side of the fog, I could spend a few millennia shooting pheasants and grouse over that muscular little springer, sharing a hamburger with him at day's end, and going to sleep each night in camp with him sprawled on top of my sleeping bag.

For now, when I take his bell and whistle down off the wall and hold them against my face, I can imagine how it's going to be.

14

"Only accurate rifles are interesting."
  – Townsend Whelen (1877-1961), rifleman, hunter, soldier, outdoorsman and writer

Project rifles

WERE IT NOT FOR a long series of project rifles, I would probably be living a comfortable retired life in Monaco, relaxing on the terrace of a palatial house overlooking the Mediterranean Sea, and wondering whether to drive the Ferrari or the Lamborghini to Paris for the weekend.

Instead, I spend much of my time in a garage workshop, glancing every now and then at the boxes of discarded rifle barrels, bolts, trigger assemblies, stocks, scope mounts, recoil pads, various parts of disassembled actions, magazines, scope mounts, springs, screws, pins, and other odds and ends.

There lies the bulk of my discretionary income from the past forty years. The rest of it has been spent on bird dogs, bird guns, hunting trips, gear, clothes, licenses, pickup trucks, and to a lesser degree, beer and cigars. So, although my children are educated and my mortgage is paid off, I was never in the market for that retirement home in the south of France.

Blame it on this expensive but worthless collection of firearm components and parts, the detritus of my project rifles – hunting rifles that did not quite meet my standards for accuracy and therefore required some upgrade and modification. That is to say, every rifle I have ever owned.

Before I explain my project rifle addiction, we should establish a definition of "accurate rifle." Craig Boddington, a gun writer whom I consider among the best in evaluating true hunting rifles, offers a practical definition of "accurate." According to Boddington, accurate is a variable term, determined by the hunting situation: the size of the animal, the range at which it is shot, the quickness with which the shot must be taken, and other factors.

For example, if you are hunting whitetail deer in northern Wisconsin woodlands a .30-30 lever-action rifle that will place a bullet within three inches of point of aim at 100 yards is "accurate." For hunting coyotes in the open grasslands of Wyoming, a .243 bolt-action rifle would have to place its bullet within three inches of point of aim at 400 yards to be considered "accurate."

Wise and sound advice and I should take heed of it. But I have evolved my own definition of accurate: "a five-shot group at 100 yards which is slightly smaller than the group the rifle will currently shoot." For example, if a new, out-of the-box, bolt-action .30-06 rifle will shoot a 1.5-inch group at 100 yards, the definition of "accurate" would be a 1.25-inch group. If the new rifle will shoot a 1.25-inch group, the definition of "accurate" would be a 1.0-inch group. And so on.

Now, it may seem that pursuing this definition of accuracy is a hopeless chase, but it does eventually reach a point of conclusion. When the rifle shoots groups smaller than 1.0 inch, I am satisfied. Well, at least for the .30 caliber, 7mm, and 6.5mm rifles. The .24 calibers should shoot groups of .75-inch and the .22 calibers should shoot groups of .50-inch, but surely that is clear and reasonable. We're talking hunting rifles and varmint rifles here, not target rifles or bench rifles. I'm not some kind of accuracy-obsessed nutcase, for heaven's sake.

Every rifle, therefore, becomes a project rifle of sorts, although some of the projects are much more challenging than others. There was a 7x57mm Spanish Mauser, for example, that was in full military stock when I got it... Well, that is too long a story, so let me illustrate my point with a simple project: the accurizing of a Ruger 10-22 semi-automatic .22 caliber rimfire rifle.

For reasons I cannot remember, I sold a perfectly good Marlin Model 881 bolt-action. 22 rifle that I had used for several years of squirrel hunting. When October came, I needed a squirrel gun and bought, on sale, a Ruger 10-22 with composite stock. Including an extra magazine, I believe the price was $167. All the .22 rifle I needed. But from the bench, it shot a 2.25-inch group at 25 yards. Lousy, even for an inexpensive squirrel rifle. I removed the barrel band, and this made the barrel more "free floating" and tightened the groups to about 2-inch. Still not nearly good enough.

The hobby of "accurizing" the Ruger 10-22 had become quite a fad in those days, so it was easy to go on-line and find hundreds of garage-mechanic gun tinkerers who would offer tips on how to solve my rifle's problems. (Looking back, I believe I could have told each one of them, "I will take your advice if you will send me $5." They were so eager to share their expertise with a novice, I think most of them would have sent me the five bucks, which would have paid at least part of the eventual cost of the project.)

On-line research and advice quickly established that the factory barrel on the Ruger 10-22 was poor quality and must be replaced as a matter of course with a heavy barrel. (This is not true, by the way; some Ruger 10-22 rifles have rough-bored barrels, but most are quite good.) Confident this would make my new rifle a tack-driver, I bought a Green Mountain heavy barrel for $107. Removing the factory barrel and installing an after-market barrel is a simple task, but a slight problem arose when I realized the heavy contour Green Mountain barrel would not fit into the factory stock.

Fortunately, the Hogue company produces an excellent "overmolded" stock with a heavy barrel channel for the Ruger 10-22. For only $68, it was a bargain. Alas, with the heavy barrel and special stock, the rifle still shot groups no better than 1.0-inch at 25 yards, and my accuracy expectations had risen to much, much greater heights by this time.

There quickly followed:
    Volquartsen trigger group assembly: $172
    Power Custom bolt, recoil spring assembly, bolt handle: $91
    Polyurethane-buffered bolt stop: $12
    Extended magazine release: $9
    Stainless steel stock bolt: $11

Installing a couple of these components required special tools, which cost about $30. Of course it was ridiculous to expect the rifle to shoot accurately without a better scope, so I bought a Leupold 3-9x40 scope for $189. Putting the whole package together required some workbench machining and tinkering, but for the most part everything went together like parts in a Swiss watch.

And – oh my god – the rifle shot beautifully: half-inch, ten-shot groups at 100 yards, if I used sub-sonic target ammo, which costs about three times as much as high-velocity .22 Long Rifle ammo.

Anyone familiar with a Ruger 10-22 will look over this project list and realize that the only factory part remaining on the rifle is the receiver housing. The flip side: if I could acquire a receiver housing, I could use the discarded factory parts to build a complete and new Ruger 10-22. But, hell, it probably wouldn't be very accurate.

So now I was the proud owner of a customized, super-accurate Ruger 10-22. For only $856. Okay, $873, if you count the sling. A semi-auto .22 rifle that shoots sub-inch groups at 100 yards. Not that I have any use for a .22 rifle that shoots sub-inch groups at 100 yards, since virtually every squirrel I shoot is about twenty yards away.

If this were an isolated incident – a random, one-time, lesson-learned project – it could be dismissed with a shrug and a sigh and the rationalization that it was less than a thousand bucks thrown away. But there were others. The aforementioned 7x57mm Mauser. A 6mm Remington on a 98 Mauser action and a Shilen barrel, with a stunningly beautiful birdseye maple stock. A Remington 700 Mountain Rifle in .30-06 that needed a few tweaks. A Savage Model 10 bolt-action in .223 caliber that needed a lot of tweaks. A Remington 700 Varmint in .223 caliber that simply had to have the stock replaced and a good scope - well, you get the idea.

The good news is that I am cured. The monkey is off my back. My most recent rifle acquisitions, a Savage Model B-II in .22 rimfire and a Savage 93 BRJ in .22 magnum, have remained factory. Totally factory. No after-market updates. No customizing. Plain Jane.

Although I think the Model B .22 would shoot slightly smaller groups if I would widen the barrel channel and free float the barrel…

15

After 25 years of use, my battered traditional-style snowshoes are still in good shape. Made of white ash and laced with rawhide, they are the Michigan or Huron model. Today's snowshoes are high-tech, with tubular aluminum frames and thermo-rubber decking, equipped with integral bindings and crampons. I can trip and fall equally well in all types and styles.

Snowshoes of white ash and rawhide

LIFE IN A NORTHERN TOWN involves a love-hate relationship with snow.

I'm not talking about those snow skiffs and sprinkles that dust the streets and lawns of more southern locales, providing residents with a day or two of holiday season décor and then melting away. No, I am talking about the parts of the country where Arctic air mass storms dump weekly deliveries of snow, December-through-March, that accumulate to 20, 30, 40, 50 inches and more. That's in the flat snowfall areas; the drifts get seriously deep.

Roads and driveways must be plowed, sidewalks must be shoveled (unless you're just made of money and can afford a snowblower), vehicles are buried under rolling mounds of white, house and garage roofs creak under the weight, and incipient avalanches overhang the eaves, patiently awaiting victims. The car is in the ditch, the front storm door is blocked, the firewood pile is entombed, and the grandchildren's sleds are lost until April. All this misery creates a certain attitude about snow: hatred.

But... this time of year is perfect for snowshoeing. When the winter gets this bad, I heartily recommend snowshoeing.

Do not go out the day of the storm, of course, unless you want to be featured in a CNN website news item illustrated with a poorly reproduced scan of your driver's license photo and the caption "stupid person" beneath it. No, wait until the storm has passed and the northern world has that "first day of the dystopian future" landscape of endless, trackless, merciless snow. Then buckle on your snowshoes and head out for a good time. Seriously.

I love snowshoeing. There was a time in my life when cross country skiing inspired fantasies of zooming over rugged snow-covered terrains, perhaps triggered by those romantic *LIFE* magazine photos of soldiers of the U.S. Army 10th Mountain Division schussing down rocky slopes on limber skis to outflank the Nazis in the Bavarian Alps, rifles and packs strapped to their backs and ski poles tucked in tight.

But my attempts to emulate them resulted in dramatic falls, even without pack and rifle, and I learned that cross country skis are not the best conveyance through second-growth woodlands in the North Country. I also learned that when you unexpectedly go over the brink of a steep slope, you are no longer cross country skiing but are instead downhill skiing — a bad choice in woodlands filled with snow-covered brush, stumps, tangles, and rocks.

Fortunately, the skis were rentals.

Snowshoeing is more my speed, figuratively and literally. When you change directions on snowshoes on a wooded slope, the moment of decision and the moment of commitment are separate; on skis, they are one and the same. When you fall down wearing snowshoes, you get back up. When you fall down wearing skis, you prepare a plan of how to get back up, and then you cautiously execute it. You may have to go to plan B.

Although you will want to don snowshoes as soon as snow accumulation makes walking in boots strenuous and tiring, perhaps only a foot or so deep, shoeing gets better and better as the snow gets deeper and deeper. Once snow depth surpasses three or four feet, most obstacles to your hike simply disappear. That includes fences, fallen trees, stumps, wild raspberry thickets, jagged rocks and boulders, and the occasional abandoned snowmobile. One the other hand, deep crevices and the edges of bluffs also disappear from sight, and you can pitch over unexpectedly.

Do not push your pace. Walk with a slow but steady gait, and stop for a few minutes rest if you become breathless or break a heavy sweat. Inhaling deep drafts of sub-zero air is not good for you. Neither is being soaking wet with sweat when you are a few miles from heated shelter on a minus 10-degree day.

I sometimes take my dogs along on a hike, but when they tire of bounding through the snow they take the easier route of walking in my snowshoe-packed trail. Every fifty yards or so, one of them will step on the tail or the rear decking of my snowshoes, forcing me to do an imitation of a drunken tap dancer attempting the buck-and-wing move on a stage covered in molasses. You may be able to remain upright. I seldom do.

More importantly, take a camera and binoculars. Best to wear a coat with large outside pockets to store these so the lenses remain snow and ice-free. Inside pockets are no good; your body heat will warm the lenses and they will steam up, then frost over when you take them out. You will want them ready, and clear-lensed, because you are going to encounter some beautiful winter scenes and, surprisingly, a lot of wildlife. Although a woodland walk on snowshoes is pretty noisy, I frequently get close to all kinds of creatures. Dozens of species of songbirds, of course, and the usual cast of squirrels, rabbits, and raccoons, but also those critters that are normally more shy and evasive: deer, turkeys, coyotes, owls, eagles, hawks.

I can't explain this. Perhaps the conversation in the winter deer yard is something like: "Hey, Ed, there's a man walking towards us about a hundred yards to the west!" "Carl, you dope, he's on snowshoes. Do you think he's going run over here and catch us?"

Snowshoeing is even more fun if your spouse and/or children go with you. Friends are okay, too, but it's a guy thing to want to play touch football on snowshoes. Wonderfully macho-camaraderie-male bonding, but hard on equipment and even harder on bodies. Friendships are not strengthened by three-mile walks on broken snowshoes with sprained knee.

So when the snow piles up this winter, get yourself a pair of snowshoes and go out into the woodlands (or the grasslands, if the wind is not too vicious) for a beautiful hike. There are thousands and thousands of acres of state, federal and county areas open to snowshoeing, and you may also know of private land you would like to walk (always ask permission).

One final tip: do not strap on bear paw style snowshoes until you have mastered the basics of the sport. Yes, they are a bit lighter and more maneuverable, but... just don't.

16

Rifle: (noun) – a firearm, usually hand-held and fired from shoulder level, having a long spirally grooved barrel intended to make a single-projectile bullet spin in flight, thereby increasing its ballistic stability and accuracy over a long distance.

Shotgun: (noun) – a firearm, usually hand-held and fired from shoulder level, having a long smooth bore barrel, that fires a charge of small bird shot, large buck shot, or a single slug at short range.

Rifled deer barrel shotgun: (compound noun) – a rifle disguised as a shotgun to comply with the convoluted deer hunting regulations developed by state legislatures and regulatory agencies.

-Definitions from North Country Dictionary *(unpublished)*

The 12 gauge .45-70 rifle

IF IT LOOKS LIKE A DUCK, walks like a duck, swims like a duck, flies like a duck, and quacks like a duck, it's a duck.

If it looks like a rifle, shoots bullets like a rifle, has sights like a rifle, and has the ballistic properties of a rifle, it's a rifle. Unless the hunting regulations of the Department of Natural Resources say it is a shotgun.

Show me a firearm with a rifled barrel and a 2-7x33mm telescopic sight, a shoulder-fired weapon that shoots a single .45-inch diameter conical projectile weighing 385 grains at 1,800 feet per second, and I will tell you it is a .45 caliber rifle. The engraving on the chamber and receiver may say it is a 12 gauge Remington Model 870 shotgun, but it is in fact a rifle.

The ballistics of the bullets fired by that rifle-barrel shotgun are identical to those of a .45-70 Government round fired from a Marlin Model 1895 lever-action, which the DNR defines as a rifle and prohibits deer hunters from using in my part of the state. To further muddy the waters, a hunter can use a handgun to hunt deer during firearm season, for example a Thompson/Center single shot pistol in .45-70 caliber with a 14-inch barrel and a scope. If he would chamber that exact same .45-70 round in a Harrington & Richardson single-shot rifle with an 18-inch barrel and open sights, and he would be in violation of the law. Go figure.

My nit-picking complaints are not, however, an argument for loosening regulations to allow the use of a wider array of rifles by the soldiers of what I call the Orange Army of Autumn. The reasoning behind the complicated DNR definition of what constitutes a shotgun and what constitutes a rifle is based, as I understand it, on the assumption that we rural residents will be safer during deer hunting season if the Orange Army troops are not spraying the countryside with high velocity, long-ranging bullets in calibers such as .30-06, .308, 7mm, .270, .243 and other "open country" deer rifles.

The DNR may be wiser than I credit. Each fall, hearing the fusillades of shots fired at running deer by some platoons of the Orange Army here in the North Country, and remembering the torrents of fire from semi-automatic rifles wielded by bands of run-and-gun coyote hunters in Nebraska, I can imagine that this rural, agrarian county on several autumn days would mimic the sounds of television news reports of street battles in Middle Eastern cities.

As much as I want to trust the safe behavior and common sense of deer hunters in my part of the country, I have witnessed too many careless and reckless acts to advocate more firepower. And looking over the gun store racks packed with those increasingly popular assault rifle-style weapons with twenty-round magazines, I fear the increasingly clueless "hunters" who arm themselves with these military small arms would rapid-fire volleys of bullets at deer on skylines, stray projectiles that fly on for hundreds of yards and pose grave danger to life and limb.

So I read the DNR firearms regulations not to be overly critical but to be entertained by the language. With the exception of a few obscure Russian novels, no literature can match the complexity and confusion of the deer hunting rules for Minnesota, Wisconsin, Iowa or any of the dozen Midwest farm states. A blend of legal-ese and administrative jargon, the regs are full of contradictory wording that plagiarizes old "Monty Python" comedy skits about petty government bureaucrats. This stuff must have been written by the same people who created the arcane screenplay for the movie *Cloud Atlas*, or perhaps by a team that analyzes obscure linguistic phrases for the CIA.

It's sort of like unraveling a code or cipher. Although college educated, I am, like most deer hunters, not a candidate for Phi Beta Kappa or Mensa, so after three or four readings of certain sections I have still not solved the acrostic riddle.

Fortunately, I can stand aloof from the confusion because my deer hunting is mostly limited to archery and muzzle-loader rifle seasons, and virtually all of it is on my own property. I may misunderstand some of the regulations but I am unlikely to violate any of them

Do not slander the DNR, deer hunters, because we have to blame ourselves for this mish-mash of rules and regulations. The Orange Armies conduct their fall maneuvers, equipped with military weapons, vehicles, cell phones, GPS units, binoculars, thermal clothing, and other gear. This introduction of evermore advanced technology into the hunt has pushed the concept of "fair chase" to the limit. We do not really hunt deer anymore; we "harvest" them.

So we may as well use the "rifle barrel shotgun." There are plenty of deer out there, and if it's not hunting, at least it is outdoor recreation.

17

O Bird Dog, companion and partner of man, when thou heareth the voice or whistle of thy master thou shalt listen and obey The Eight Commandments.

The Eight Commandments

RICK SMITH, a professional dog trainer that I regard as one of the best in the business, has said that a bird dog only has to respond to three commands to be a good hunter. The dog has to come to you, go with you, and be still.

For some bird dog owners that is probably true. In the field, if a pointing dog will go where you want to go, come when you call, and "whoa" on command, you can have a successful day's hunt. That is assuming the dog has the talent and desire to do what comes naturally: cover the ground, use its nose, point, stand staunch, and retrieve.

What else does the dog need to know, really?

For a hunter who owns a dozen or more pointers and setters and hunts bobwhite quail on plantation fields in the Old South or the wide open spaces of Texas or Oklahoma, I suppose that is true. I have taken part in a few of those hunts, and it is impressive to see those high-powered, hard-running pointers cover the ground, two pair down, four more pair waiting in the crates on the truck for their turn. The hunters follow, riding on a high-clearance four-wheel-drive rig, climbing down to take shotguns from the rack when the dogs locate a covey.

Come evening, the dogs are checked nose-to-tail (and especially feet) for cuts and scrapes, brushed, fed, and put back into their kennel runs out-of-sight and out-of-mind until the next day's hunt. Just like the four-wheel-drive truck.

Most of us do not hunt birds in that classic plantation style, and we have a different type of relationship with the one or two bird dogs we own. Our dogs are less "employee" and more "family." We hunt our dogs three or four months of the year, but we live with them twelve months a year. So I advise tyro owner-trainers to teach the commands that will assure they have a dog they can both hunt over and live with.

Your life with dogs in the field and in the home will be more enjoyable and much less frustrating if your dog will honor The Eight Basic Commands: *Come, Whoa, Sit, Hie-On, Fetch, Give, Kennel-Up*, and *Be Quiet*. The dog must not only recognize the commands but also obey them, unfailingly.

There are a few more "citizenship" commands that every dog learns early on. *No* and *Get Down*, for example, are part of training from about eight weeks of age. If you have the same redneck roots as me, you will also use several command words that are not found in any dictionary, words such as *Nyarn* and *Dairnt-Yoo* and of course *GIT!* All indispensable for behavior modification sessions.

For field work you will teach your dog several other commands that will help it become the best hunting partner it can be. You will want to train the dog to obey the words *Heel, Get Back, Over, Hunt Dead, Go Easy, Leave It*, and perhaps a few more terms the two of you work out for better teamwork. By the time your dog is in its third or fourth hunting season, you two will have developed a twenty or thirty word vocabulary of cooperation.

Remember, you are not having a dialog with your dog, you are giving orders. Dogs do not speak English, not even the English breeds (although I once knew a border collie that was fairly fluent in both Scots-Gaelic and Italian.) And they cannot understand the convoluted human reasoning behind your instructions. They act based on word recognition and conditioning.

I do have a hunting buddy who carries on continual conversation with his dog, Missy, while hunting and she seems to enjoy this. Not that it in any way affects her actions, but it keeps her informed about his location in heavy cover and encourages her to think that he is working the birds to her satisfaction. As far as command words, he has but one: *Goddammitmissy!* Depending on inflection, resonance, volume, and tonal emphasis, it seems to serve for a dozen of my command words, but not being as perceptive and intuitive as Missy, I cannot always determine which one.

Both effusive praise and stern lecture do have their place, however, in the training and obedience game. A dog has two motivations for obeying instructions: desire for reward and fear of punishment. (Exactly the same as humans, now that I think about it.) Many's the time I have grabbed a dog by the collar when it has intentionally and knowingly disregarded an order, and I excel in giving scoldings more degrading and scathing than any sermon delivered by an Irish parish priest.

On the opposite side of the coin, the training word I use a hundred times more frequently than any of The Eight Basic Commands is the phrase that gets the absolute best response:

GOOD DOG!

18

Bluebell had been saying that he knew the men hated us for raiding their crops and gardens, and Toadflax answered, "That wasn't why they destroyed the warren. It was just because we were in their way. They killed us to suit themselves."
    -*from* Watership Down *by Richard Adams (b. 1920)*

Rabbitat

COTTONTAIL RABBITS that live on our place have a cozy deal.

They have shelter in the woods, they raid the garden all summer and early autumn, they eat discarded greens from the compost pile after the hard freezes of late fall, and they nibble bark from young trees and feast under the bird feeders through the winter. Posh accommodations for rodents.

In exchange, they let our two bird dogs chase them around the perimeter of the yard three or four minutes each morning when they first get out of their kennel runs. Neither Sasha nor Abbey has ever caught a rabbit, but they take great joy in the pursuit. And for some reason, perhaps an anthropomorphic empathy created by reading *Watership Down*, we like having the rabbits here.

Yes, replanting rows of beans that have been eaten down by the bunnies is more than an annoyance, but we do like to sit on the deck on a warm summer evening and watch them socialize, dance, scuffle, nuzzle, and feed (in the woods, not the garden). We do not pretend to truly understand how each piece of the wildlife puzzle fits into nature's grand drama on our farm, but we want the rabbits to remain actors on the stage, the same as the redtail hawks, deer, foxes, crows, toads, moles, rat snakes, coyotes, the dozens of types of song birds – all the thousands of species that play roles in the production.

Maintaining suitable environment for the rabbits requires some effort on our part, more than you might think. They may be an invasive pest in Australia, but in the North Country of the upper Midwest their numbers have been declining. Their habitat has diminished as farms have become huge tracts of agricultural industrial land bathed in herbicides, insecticides, anhydrous ammonia fertilizers, and other chemical poisons.

Our own woodlands have become less beneficial to wildlife over the past thirty years as the hardwood trees have grown tall and canopied, shading out the undergrowth. A mature northern forest is a beautiful place for a morning walk and a contemplative setting for deep thoughts about life and purpose, but it is not the best environment for most wild species, certainly not for cottontail rabbits. Fortunately for them (and me), I have been able to offset some of this habitat loss through the creation of dozens of brush piles that my wife calls "rabbitat."

Most rabbitat on our farm is a by-product of cutting dead trees, some for firewood, some to clear driveways and paths, and some to bring down the "widow makers": toppled trees that are caught in the branches of adjacent trees, awaiting their Murphy's Law moment to come crashing down. Elms are prolific but doomed trees in our part of the world. Dutch elm disease infects virtually all elms when they reach about twenty-four inches girth, and they die slowly over the next several years. Forlorn skeletons standing here and there in our woods, these dead elms shed their bark and small branches over the course of a couple harsh winters, and then they are ready for their ultimate destiny in the wood stove.

Once felled, the trunks are cut into foot-long sections and stacked to await the splitting maul. Actually, in my senior years, they await the hydraulic splitting machine. The larger limbs are also cut into stove-sized lengths and hauled directly to the woodpile. The small limbs and branches – and the snarled tangle of wild grapevine, creeper, bark, and other "junk" – gets tossed into a pile during the process. Perfect rabbitat.

Do not make a pile the size of your kitchen table, a shelter too small to protect a rabbit family from even mild weather and no safeguard at all from predators. Make the pile the size of your kitchen, or bigger. A two-tree pile is good. A three-tree pile is better. A four-tree pile is excellent.

Come spring, avoid that arsonist's urge to set a match to these brush piles. For some reason, city folk seem to think a brush pile in the woods is a blemish. I think it is a beauty mark. The more the better. There are at least a dozen on our place, and they provide habitat for many species of wildlife, not just the rabbits.

One cool October evening a couple years ago, while I was watching the rabbits socializing on the "porch" of their rabbitat brush pile east of the house, an unexpected, nostalgic memory of rabbit hunting as a ten-year-old boy filled my mind. I was briefly tempted to get the .22 rifle and pick off a cottontail bunny or two for the stew pot. But I couldn't do it.

There I sat, cup of hot coffee in hand, watching the last shadows of evening fade away to darkness, quietly enjoying this moment of autumn beauty and wonder in a world that seems to have fewer and fewer such moments. And that, I thought, is probably what the rabbits are doing, too.

I have my comfortable and secure habitat, they have theirs. Let's savor it for a peaceful hour.

Tomorrow morning, Sasha and Abbey can chase you rabbits all around the brush piles again.

19

I did not mind killing anything, any animal, if I killed it cleanly. They all had to die and my interference with the nightly and seasonal killing that went on all the time was very minute and I had no guilty feeling at all.
    - from the novel Green Hills of Africa *by Ernest Hemingway (1899-1961)*

Shoulder to the wheel

LIKE MY DIMINISHING ABILITY to drink and enjoy single malt whiskey, my ability to draw and shoot a bow has declined over the years. As a fellow hunter has observed, "Shooting is a perishable skill."

Indeed.

Drawing and shooting a bow requires much cooperative work of various anatomical groups, a collaborative effort that the labor force of my aging body is no longer willing to perform – especially that renegade Union of Muscle Mechanics and Synapse Transmitters in my right shoulder. They seldom speak to one another these days, after the bitter split caused by two rotator cuff tears.

Rehabilitation is not necessarily reconciliation in the world of chiropractics.

A bow hunter's shoulder injury woes are exacerbated through the years by the natural decline in muscle mass and strength associated with aging. This is not so evident standing on the archery range on a warm summer afternoon, shooting a dozen arrows into a six-inch circle target at twenty-five yards and pretending you still have the skill of a thirty-year-old. But on a late fall evening, with the temperature below freezing, your body twisted in odd angles in a tree stand, there will be no smooth draw-lock-release sequence to your shot.

There may not even be a draw. My old Browning bow has been adjusted down, down, down in draw weight from 65 to 60 to 55 to 50 pounds over the past decade. Even at 50 pounds I cannot reliably bring my release hand to my anchor point (knuckle of right thumb on the hinge of the jawbone). Sometimes it requires significant upper body torque and twist to pull back the bowstring, motion that alarms any deer in range and sends it running to find safer trails in the woods.

Three years ago I risked a shot at a doe that had been startled by my herky-jerky draw movement. I released quickly, and the arrow hit too high and too far back. After a twenty-minute wait I tracked her two hours in the dark, finding the arrow almost at once but trailing more and more slowly as I found ever-smaller drops of blood in the glare of the headlamp. The next morning I picked up the trail and followed it another two hours, helped by my wife who is a far better tracker than I am.

We never found the doe. She probably survived, I tell myself. The arrow wound had ceased to bleed a quarter mile before we gave up. But it was the worst wounded animal experience of my hunting life.

Although I have long accepted that killing is part of hunting, I have not been able to fully adopt Hemingway's philosophy that in nature killing is incessant and remorseless and my part of it is insignificant. When I become dispassionate about killing a deer, or nonchalant about wounding a deer, I will stop bow hunting.

The following summer I faced a choice: give up bow hunting or apply for a special permit that would allow me to hunt with a crossbow because of my incapacitated shoulder. After much mental wrangling on ethics, I chose the latter.

The archery salesman at the sporting goods store assured me that I would love hunting with a crossbow and that it would be as enjoyable as hunting with my old compound bow. I have not found this to be true. If I had my way, I would greatly prefer to go back to the compound bow. This has more to do with the aesthetic of bow hunting than the ethical issues.

One of the joys of bow hunting is that it is minimalist: you and a three-pound bow and a quiver with a few arrows make for a quiet and inconspicuous time in a tree stand in the woodlands. The crossbow, in comparison, is heavy and cumbersome and demands constant handling. It bumps into things and is noisy. Cocking it requires a separate cord. Carrying it requires a sling.

Shooting a compound bow (or a recurve bow or long bow) is a graceful athletic feat. Shooting a crossbow is a mechanical skill, much like shooting a rifle.

Subjectively, I think a crossbow has a crude appearance while a recurve bow, longbow, or even a compound bow has artistry and beauty in its form. I compare it to the difference between a helicopter and an airplane. Or in the case of recurve or long bows, an aerobatic glider or sailplane. Yes, helicopters are functional, perhaps more functional than gliders, but they are such ugly machines.

Nevertheless, here we are. To date, I have taken four deer with a crossbow, and the venison has been just as tasty and nourishing as that from previous deer. A friend suggested I would be able to shoot deer at much longer range with a crossbow than with a compound, but that is a non-issue on my heavily wooded hunting grounds. The deer killed with the crossbow have been shot at nine yards, eleven yards, fourteen yards, and seven yards, pacing from the tree stand to the place where the crossbow bolt was found jutting out of the ground after penetrating through the deer. Those are the same distances at which I typically took deer with my old compound bow.

Humanely, I have not found the crossbow to be any more nor any less lethal than the compound bow. However I am much more confident of placing my shot in a vital spot with the crossbow. And that is why I use it.

The hunt itself – well, if you are a bow hunter you know it has rewards and enjoyments that no other form of hunting offers. If you are not a bow hunter, you are missing out on a wonderful and spiritual outdoor experience, and you should try it. This fall.

20

Good decisions are based on experience. Experience is based on bad decisions.
  – Clement Seagrave

Good decisions

YOU HAVE HEARD that old saying: Experience is a great teacher. What a lie! Experience is a lousy teacher.

What kind of teacher would give you the final exam first and then present the course syllabus and materials later, after you have failed abysmally? That old saying should be, "Experience is a cruel teacher." The kind of teacher that believes all learning must be accompanied by pain and suffering. And injury, for the advanced lessons.

Experience, for the bird hunter, is more like outdoor classes in practical physics taught by the college of hard knocks. We learn more than we ever wanted to know about gravity, navigation, time, ballistics, friction, metallurgy, and electronics. We also get a crash course in weather forecasting, with emphasis on the effects of wind, rain and temperature on rocks and water.

As a bonus, the college offers us hands-on instruction in first aid (human and canine), entomology (tick removal for extra credit), herpetology (focus on venomous snakes species), wilderness survival (a poncho can save your life), food poisoning (toilet paper should always be in the pocket of your hunting vest), and allergic reactions (antihistamines work best if taken with bourbon).

Outside of our major area of study, we are required to take elective courses in social skills: classes that teach prudent behavior, appropriate alcohol use, clothing selection, table manners, how to tell time, when and how to use a telephone, and coping with (deserved) verbal and physical abuse from an irate spouse. I'm not sure which part of the curriculum deals with skunks, porcupines and badgers, but it's in there somewhere. After several tries, I finally got passing grades in all three.

Learning outdoor skills through experience is a long and arduous process, and many a bird hunter has given up before achieving his APP&WD Certification (Acumen, Prescience, Prudence & Wise Discretion), the equivalent of the doctoral degree in the hunter's world. It is dispiriting to meet one of these fellows who has neglected his education. More than a few times I have encountered the non-degreed hunter deep in the woods, bewildered and on the edge of panic, who has asked "Do you have a compass?" Do I have *A* compass? As in one, singular compass? No, I have three compasses, any one of which I am willing to sell for $50. I will also have two topographical maps of the area, $100 for the spare one.

I have learned that higher education not only adds to the quality of one's life but also provides certain financial benefits.

All six of the charter members of my bird hunting group – commonly known as the Over The Hill Gang – have been awarded the APP&WD Certification at least twenty years ago. If the Goddess of Wisdom and her handmaiden Perspicacity were to bestow the honor of immortal fame upon the world's most experientially sophisticated bird hunter by placing him in the heavens as a constellation, we six shall surely be among the final starry candidates. Well, all except for Dave who gets lost in the woods a couple times each fall.

Knowing this, and aware of our opportunity to share our knowledge and legerdemain with the greater hunting fraternity, I mentioned to the OTH Gang that we should launch a website with weekly tips and bits of lore that could speed an outdoorsman's practical education and spare him the pain, anguish and embarrassment of stumbling through the string of mishaps and disasters that we suffered over the years. Imagine my chagrin when they told me, to a man, "Hell no! Let them learn things the hard way, just like we did."

Nevertheless, I plan to open a school of hunter education. Ever the literary entrepreneur, I hope to offer correspondence and online courses leading to the aforesaid APP&WD Certification. The modest tuition will include a tasteful diploma for framing and mounting, and a patch to sew on your hunting vest. Maybe a compass and a whistle, too.

Here is a ten question, multiple choice test that will be typical of the course material.

Appropriate Behavior, Decision-Making, and Etiquette for the Aspiring Bird Hunter

1. You shoot a 16 gauge shotgun and are selecting ammunition for a hunt 300 miles from home. You should pack:

A. One box of 16 gauge shotshells size 7½ and one box size 6
B. One box of 16 gauge shells in each shot size in the cabinet
C. Two boxes of 16 gauge shells in each shot size in the cabinet
D. Every box of 16 gauge shotshells in the cabinet

2. You are choosing footwear for a woodcock hunt in a nearby state and have been assured by the locals that the marshes are all dry this year. You should:

A. Pack a pair of ankle-high rubber boots
B. Pack a pair of knee-high rubber boots
C. Pack a pair of hip boots
D. Pack A, B, and C

3. You are drinking beer with friends and reliving the day's hunt when, at 10 p.m., you remember you promised your wife you would call her at 6 p.m. You should:

A. Decide to call her in the morning
B. Call her immediately and apologize
C. Call her and crinkle paper against your cell phone while you shout, "Is this connecting? I've been trying to call you four hours!"
D. Wait until 1 a.m., then call and say, "Oh my god! I never thought I'd hear your voice again! Let me tell you what happened…"

4. Throughout a day's grouse hunt, your dog has performed magnificently while the dogs of your hunting companions have performed poorly. You should brag about your dog:

A. During the day's hunt
B. In the evening following the hunt, after drinks
C. A month after hunting season ends
D. One year after the dog has gone to its eternal reward

5. You have had a great day of quail shooting, cleanly killing twelve birds with twelve shots from your 28 gauge gun. You should mention this to your hunting companions:

A. Only after one of them commends you on your fine shooting
B. Only after all of them commend you on your fine shooting
C. Only if one of them specifically asks about your bag and the number of shells
D. Never

6. Your hunting companion has just shot a rare double on woodcock. As he turns to look at you with a beaming smile, you should quickly:

A. Turn your back to him and whistle for your dog
B. Remove your glasses and pretend to clean them
C. Congratulate him on his lucky shooting and ask if this is his first-ever double
D. Break open your gun and ask, "Oh, did you shoot, too?"

7. Your hunting companion has arrived at camp with a new, expensive over-under shotgun. You should:

A. Compliment him on his wise choice of a fine gun
B. Mention you read an article about this gun's unreliability
C. Have him mount the gun several times and tell him it does not fit him correctly
D. Ask if his wife knows how much he paid for it

8. You and a hunting companion have come to a beaver-dammed creek that you must cross to get into grousey-looking cover. Before wading, you should:

A. Throw a stick across and tell your dog to fetch
B. Throw a stick across and tell his dog to fetch
C. Test the water depth by probing with the barrels of your gun
D. Test the water depth by probing with the barrels of his gun

9. In December, the two of you come to the same creek, which is now frozen over and you must cross on the ice. You should:
   A. Let him cross first
   B. Let him cross first
   C. Let him cross first
   D. Let him cross first

10. On a pheasant hunt, everyone in camp shoots a limit of birds the first day except for you, who missed three easy shots. You should:
   A. Pout silently and drink everyone else's beer
   B. Pout silently and drink everyone else's scotch
   C. Pout silently and drink everyone else's bourbon
   D. Do A, B, and C

Please submit your answers by postal mail with $10 enclosed to cover the cost of grading and return postage. You must answer at least seven of the questions correctly to receive academic credit toward APP&WD Certification. This is an open-book test, and you can find the answers in my novel, *Hunting Birds*, available in paperback and Kindle editions at amazon.com.

21

Based on the Russian troika folk dance but performed one-legged with extemporaneous free-form interpretations, the squck polka ends with a lively whoop-and-sploosh maneuver in black, soupy goo.

Squck

SOME YEARS in the North Country the end of winter is a door slammed shut. One day the high temperature is three below zero, the next day it's 52 above.

Three to four feet of accumulated snow and ice melt in less than a week, and the icy torrents of water fill the dry runs between the bluffs, flood the creeks, and swell the rivers to overflowing. It is a beautiful time of year, although a bit treacherous as ice hides just below an inch or two of soft surface. I love to sit on the deck in the late afternoon, cup of hot coffee in hand, listening to the meltwater race and roar through the draws on the east and south sides of the house.

Clearly, winter has ended, but spring has not really arrived. Except for the drifts and hard-packed driveway edges, the snow and ice are quickly disappearing, and the last of the icicles have dropped from the eaves to plunge spear-like into the thawing turf. But no shoots of green are emerging from the ground, trees are not budding out, that fragrant waft of spring scent is not in the air, and the dogs are not shedding their winter coats.

No longer winter, but, unfortunately, not yet spring. We have entered that North Country transition season that I call squck, so named because wherever I walk my feet sink into the water-mud-ice-snow mix that covers the farm, and each step is accompanied by the squck sound of rubber boot pulling away from the suction of the swampy ground. On afternoon walks, the tread of running dogs provides an double-time "splat-a-splat" accompaniment and a heavy spray of muddy water that accounts for the speckled look of my clothes and face this time of year.

Occasionally, my foot pulls completely out of the boot, cueing the exciting and energetic squck polka, based on the Russian troika folk dance but performed one-legged with extemporaneous free-form interpretations. It ends with a lively whoop-and-sploosh maneuver in black, soupy goo that leaves me with a sodden sock to be forced reluctantly back into the boot for a squishy walk home. Over my many years of squck polka dancing I have accumulated an assortment of gray-and-black, two-tone wool socks that mystify my friends who live south of the squck zone.

Despite the cherished memories of these fun times, squck is not my favorite season.

For one thing, as the snow cover melts away it reveals things that I have been able to put out of my mind for the past four months. The most obvious and noisome are the 1,097 piles of dog pooh, some in places that defy reason. Why did Abbey decide to climb up there to dump out? And how did she do it? Watch your step: squck is pooh patrol time.

Branches blown down from trees by winter storms create a complicated squck game of pick-up-sticks, pace increasing as we get closer and closer to the first day of lawn mowing.

Also gradually emerging from the snow are the grandchildren's sleds (didn't I put those in the garage before the January 8th snowstorm?), the scoop shovel (so that's where it is!), a pliers, a pair of five-buckle boots, a trailer hitch pin, a soggy box of wooden matches, a flashlight, a mouse-chewed chore glove, a coiled electrical extension cord, a wood-splitting maul, and a mesh bag containing a dog training whistle, two retrieving dummies, a nylon lead, and a half-dozen mushy dog treats.

I call these things "squck gifts."

Washing the car and pickup could be a daily chore during squck, since every trip on gravel roads applies a coating of gritty slop to vehicles, tapering from a quarter-inch thick at the roofline to more than an inch on the rocker panels. All residents of squck country have accent slashes of light brown on the backs of their pant legs where they rub against car door sills while exiting or entering. Since car washing is hopeless until April, everyone's vehicles become a uniform gray-brown color for a few weeks. Out-of-towners are easy to spot, driving around in cars of odd colors such as red, blue, green...

Squck is also the time of odor emergence. The compost pile that has been steaming unseen beneath three feet of snow, the manure mound behind the barn, the deer carcass on the edge of the bluff, the rotten round bale at the top of the driveway – all these will burst into olfactory notice. So will the knit hats, gloves, scarves, facemasks, and sweaters jammed into the wooden box in the mud room or entryway.

The least of squck annoyances, unless you lean your hand on one by accident, are the wasps that emerge too early, somehow find their way into the house, and perch on window ledges to warm themselves in the sunshine. The few surviving Asian beetles and box elder bugs come out to sing their swan song, too.

Then comes the change to Daylight Savings Time so we can have the joy of getting out of bed in the pre-dawn darkness for a few more days.

Squck. It makes me grumpy as a bear. I wonder if bears hibernate through squck. If not, I know what makes them so damned grumpy in the spring.

22

I was twelve years old the first time I ever shot a bird on the wing over a pointing dog, and it was by far the best thing that had ever happened in my life. I still remember standing there shaking because I was so excited to have shot a honest-to-god ruffed grouse in the rainy popple and cedar woods on a cold morning. The smell and taste of the gun smoke was in my nose and mouth, and my ears were still ringing from the sound of the shot, and a wet orange-and-white Brittany spaniel was handing me the dead bird, and I was thinking that heaven must be just like this.
  - from the novel Hunting Birds – The Lives and Legends of the Pine County Rod, Gun, Dog and Social Club

One good dog

A BIRD HUNTER only gets one good dog in his lifetime.

I've heard that old saw a hundred times. Not sure how it ever got started or why anyone thinks it's true, but every now and then I'll still meet another bird hunter in the field, ask him about his dog, and hear something like, "Oh, he's not so good, but I had a really good dog about twenty years ago, and you know you only get one good bird dog in your lifetime."

Really? Over the past forty years I've had four, and the puppy I started this season also promises to be a good one.

Admittedly, I have had three mediocre bird dogs and two poor ones. The mediocre ones had their good days and their bad days, contributing to my understanding of canine behavior, improving my whistle-blowing skills, and enriching my vocabulary. Neither of the poor ones was kept on the roster for a second season, but both made nice pets – for someone else.

Finding a good bird dog is not difficult. Training one, from a well-bred puppy, is only slightly more difficult. So where did this "one good dog in a lifetime" nonsense come from?

My best guess is that it has little to do with a shortage of good bird dogs and a lot to do with a shortage of bird hunters who are willing to invest the time, self-discipline, and money into acquiring, training and handling a hunting dog. Somewhere along the line, these hunters stumble into a dog that trains itself, more or less, to tag along in the field, find some birds, and perhaps even retrieve the ones knocked down. Hey! Presto! The old "one good dog" adage is validated, and the hunter can spend the rest of his life with bad ones, knowing that he has had his share of good fortune in canines.

That's a shame for the hunter, of course, who does not get to enjoy the full richness of upland bird hunting. The epitome of a day afield is the opportunity to be part of that wonderful dog-hunter-gamebird choreography that culminates with the perfect find, perfect point, perfect shot, and perfect retrieve. It's an even greater misfortune for the many upland bird dogs – pointing breeds and flushing breeds – that had the genetic traits and the drive to be good or even great in the field but never had the opportunity to achieve their potential.

I was enchanted the first time I ever saw this dog-hunter teamwork, almost forty-five years ago on a pheasant hunt among the shelterbelts and plum thickets of northeast Nebraska. I vowed I would find myself a fine Labrador retriever and we would become a fearsome pheasant hunting team. In fact, it took many a year to learn how to do this. I did finally mesh gears with a fine English springer spaniel, but I had to first overcome much canine misinformation foisted upon me in my youth.

Bird dogs were not common among my many uncles and older cousins, the men I admired as hunters when I was growing up in a rural community in Ohio. A few had coon dogs, and one had an ill-tempered cocker spaniel of dubious bird hunting ability, but for the most part their "bird dogs" were the same farm dogs that herded cows into the milking parlor and caught rats in the barn. They were all mixed-breed curs, big and smelly and dopey and out of control, and I loved them.

Consequently, I was slow in learning the Great Secret. To spare you much frustration and wasted time, I will share with you that Great Secret: GET A GOOD DOG.

That seems simple enough, doesn't it? The Great Secret will not, by itself, produce a great upland bird dog, but it is the absolutely essential prerequisite. You will still have to be disciplined in spending the time and energy to teach the dog the eight basic obedience commands it must learn so that you can both live with it and hunt with it: Come, Sit (or Hup or Whoa), Hie On, Fetch, Give, Heel, Kennel, Be Quiet. You can add more, of course. One hunting buddy taught his Brittany to put the retrieved bird into the game pouch of his hunting vest, which I thought was a pretty nifty trick until the day the dog put a lightly wounded rooster pheasant in there, which resulted in much dancing, shouting, barking, running, and a nasty puncture wound from a spur.

Getting back to the Great Secret, I am going to assume you want to get a puppy and train it yourself, which is an enormously rewarding adventure that has the added benefit of making the dog the best teammate and companion it can be. You would be wise to read a few dog training books before you get the puppy. I still like the Richard Wolters *Gun Dog* book and its spin-offs (*Water Dog, Game Dog*, etc.) and the James Spencer *Point!* and *Hup!* books, but there are several good ones out there. There are several good DVDs, too, but I'm an old-school trainer who likes to have the book.

The choice of breed is up to you. I'll suggest that you make a careful evaluation of the types of bird hunting you do, and then make the decision on whether you want a flushing breed or a pointing breed. If you are primarily a quail hunter, do not get a Chesapeake Bay retriever. If you are primarily a duck hunter, do not get an English setter. Beyond that simplistic advice, I'm not making any recommendations. There are excellent dogs in all the bird hunting breeds.

Do a lot of research on the Internet and make a lot of phone calls to find the breeder from whom you will buy your puppy. Personally, I like smaller operations where the dogs get a lot of love and attention from the kennel owners, and the puppies are in an environment that assures they will be mentally and emotionally sound as well as physically sound. On the other hand, I avoid backyard breeders because they usually have litters produced by "my good dog, Emma, and my buddy's good dog, Sledge, so these puppies will be first-class bird dogs." Probably not.

Pick a breeder that has been in business for a while and knows a lot about lineage and genetics. Don't be shy about calling hunters who have previously purchased dogs from that breeder, and ask about their experiences.

You will pay somewhere between $800 and $1,500 for a good puppy. Maybe more. Does that make you choke? Well then, go spend your money on bowling or golf. If you buy a cheap dog, you are almost certainly getting a bad prospect. You'll waste two or three years before you give up hope it will ever be a worthwhile bird dog – and then understand why it's wise to spend $1,000 on a good one.

Three or four or five years from now, you will take that dog afield and experience that magical sequence: perfect find, perfect point (or flush), perfect retrieve. At that moment, you'll realize you have a good bird dog, maybe a great bird dog. And it won't be your last. You can have more than one. Many more.

23

White elm burns like rotten mold;
Flames that sputter low and cold.
Red elm burns both hot and bright;
A steady fire all through the night.
         - Clement Seagrave

Red elm

TO HEAT YOUR HOME with a wood stove, you have to enjoy cutting and splitting wood.

Oh, you might get by for a year or two on the fallacious belief that you are befriending the forest eco-system, or the erroneous idea that there is economic benefit in heating with wood rather than fossil fuels. But to keep at it for year after year, twenty or thirty years, you're going to have to really like the heavy work of cutting and splitting and hauling and stacking firewood.

Love it, in fact. Do it not as a noisome ritual of September and October, but as a fun and rewarding labor of love. Recreation. Play time.

Otherwise, you are going to ditch the wood heat experiment after a winter or two, except for lighting a token fire in the stove for atmosphere when friends visit. You'll nibble cheese and crackers and sip glasses of full-bodied red wine (a good complement to oak or maple wood smoke), while out in the woodshed ($1,600), the mice and rust nibble away at your chainsaw ($500), log chains ($175), axe ($49), splitting maul ($57), hydraulic wood splitter ($1,100), and various accessories ($200-$1,000). We'll let you pretend that the four-wheeler ATV, heavy duty hauling cart, steel-toe boots, hard hat, hearing protectors, leather work gloves, and safety glasses were purchased for other purposes than the firewood project and can be removed from the debit sheet. So, amortized over the next ten years, you're paying only about $50 per dose of cozy woodstove ambience.

Fortunately, I do love cutting firewood. And splitting it. I have learned to like hauling and stacking, but those will never match the torrid love affair I have with my Stihl chainsaw and splitting mauls. When we bought our 130-year-old farm house and surrounding woodlots, I rushed madly, recklessly into the relationship. Yes, I have paid in pain and suffering for my impetuosity and passion, but it has been worth it. No regrets.

My playground is my back yard. Literally. Our acreage is a woodland clumsily and wantonly logged in the 1970s and destructively grazed by cattle in the 1980s. Neglected and unused for a decade it regenerated in stands of fast-growing trees: box elder, elm, soft maple, aspen, plum, wild cherry – densely interspersed with red cedar, prickly ash, wild raspberry, gooseberry, and bountiful burdock. Tender stems of oak, walnut, hickory, hard maple, ash, butternut and other hardwood species also emerged from the forest floor, but most were devoured by deer and rabbits. The "undesirable" tree species were unmolested and thrived.

Especially the elms. At least until their bark grew sufficiently thick to attract *Hylurgopinu rufipes*, the elm bark beetle, which bores into the tree and infects it with *Ophiostoma novo-ulmi*, commonly known as Dutch elm disease. This virulent fungus kills the tree over the course of several years through a sort of auto-immune reaction that results in self-strangulation. It does not, however, send the elm species spiraling into extinction, as the chestnut blight exterminated the American chestnut tree, because during their ten to fifteen years of life the elms shower down thousands of seeds (encased in those wonderful 'helicopter' seed pods) and spike up 'suckers' from their root systems, procreating future generations of trees – which will soon contract the insect-borne fungus and begin their slow death.

Over a forty-year period, about 1960-2000, Dutch elm disease killed hundreds of thousands – perhaps millions? – of the magnificent elm trees that shaded the parks and streets of eastern and Midwestern towns. The ten to fifteen-year life of the elm tree has made it a species of no economic value, except as firewood.

The hardwood trees of my woodlands have now matured, canopied, and shaded out much of the undergrowth. Dozens of dead elms stand naked of bark, awaiting a strong wind to bring them down to their ultimate destination: my woodstove. A rough inventory suggests there will be sufficient firewood for another twenty years, longer than I will be physically able to harvest it.

But there is elm, and then there is elm. More specifically, there is white elm, also called American elm, *ulmus Americana*; and there is red elm, also called slippery elm, *ulmus rubra*.

The two species both have the twisted, spiraling grain that makes them difficult to split. But the similarity ends there. After a few years of heating with wood, you can distinguish white elm from red elm at a glance, but even if you could not, the character of the wood reveals itself with the first bite of the chainsaw. White elm is butter, red elm is iron.

White elm is firewood only in the sense that it does burn and produce fire and some heat. Plentiful in my woodlands (white elms outnumber red elms by a factor of about eight-to-one), it is also plentiful in my woodpile because when a white elm comes down it usually has to be cut up and removed to plant an oak or walnut or maple seedling in its place. In my stove, small splits of white elm burn fast, produce relatively little heat, and leave much ash. Big splits have to be coaxed to burn at all, with flue wide open, and the sputtering flames produce barely enough heat to bring to boil the teapot atop the stove.

Red elm is the ne plus ultra of firewood. Hard and heavy, even small splits burn for hours, producing huge numbers of BTUs. Big splits burn hot and steady through the night, leaving a generous bed of glowing coals to rekindle the fire in the morning. One cord of red elm is worth four cords of white. When I find a red elm fallen, or ready to be felled, there is much celebration.

And in addition to the joy it brings me, this firewood hobby (obsession? passion?) heats my home for free. Well, for minimal cost. Less than LP gas, anyway. Probably. I'll do the numbers later. For now, I'm warming my feet by the woodstove.

24

The clay target game is good practice. In fact, if one can explore it from all its angles, it is the best available practice. It teaches timing, lead, angle of flight, and all the seemingly necessary functions of mind and body, but it is still not bird shooting.
    - from Drummer in the Woods *by Burton L. Spiller (1886-1973)*

Clay target games

TO BECOME A GOOD WING-SHOT, to master the art and science of shooting a bird in flight, you must learn and practice by shooting one or more of the clay target games: trap, skeet, sporting clays, five stand, and a dozen other lesser-known.

In my part of the country, a bird hunter may have been able to become a first-class shotgunner a hundred years ago when the short grass prairies teemed with sharptail grouse and the brushy waterways supported peak populations of bobwhite quail. In that golden era, he might shoot at hundreds of birds on the wing each year. Even today a shotgunner, at least a wealthy shotgunner, can travel to Central or South American counties where he can shoot at unlimited numbers of doves and waterfowl.

But the vast majority of bird hunters are going to shoot at fewer than a hundred birds on the wing each season, and that is far too few to sharpen or maintain the motor skills of wing-shooting. To do that, you must spend some time on clay target courses.

How much time? How many targets? That depends on your level of athletic ability, reaction time, reflexes, eyesight. For me, a shooter who is average in all those categories, it requires a minimum of a thousand clay targets a year. Any less than that and I can expect to have a frustrating year of shooting afield.

Every so often I hear stories of some bird hunter who is a "natural," a gunner who hits every bird at which he points a shotgun, and of course he has never shot a clay target in his life. I have met only one of these naturals in the flesh when a couple of his friends coaxed him out to the gun club to humiliate all us skeet shooters. As I remember, he broke fourteen of twenty-five targets on his first round. He did a bit worse on his second round. Chastened but not converted, one of his friends insisted, "That's on these clay targets. He never misses anything with feathers on it."

Well, we all have our own level of pride.

I will agree with this truism: clay target shooting is NOT bird shooting. Almost all the clay target games were created as practice sessions for wing-shots during the off-season. None is perfect practice. Far from it. But they are the best substitute we have, and we are wise to make use of them.

Shooting the clay target games teaches, or reinforces, the skills of target acquisition, good gun mounting and pointing, timing, tracking, lead, trigger pull, and follow-though. In short, the target games train your body to perform as one with the shotgun.

Baseball, tennis, golf – all require a complicated and coordinated use of your sensory and motor functions to hit the ball. Wing-shooting is much the same. It cannot be performed in a one-two-three-four cadence; it must be automatic, smooth, continuous, flowing, and consistent. Some shooting coaches preach that your eyes and hands must work in conjunction to guide the gun muzzle to the flight path of the target. This is not strictly true; your entire body must work in conjunction to guide the gun muzzle to the flight path of the target.

This is achieved by learning good shooting form, and then training your body to carry out that good form on every shot. It requires repetition and repetition and repetition. And more repetition. Oddly, a golfer who is also a shotgunner will hit thousands of balls at a driving range every year, repetition to perfect his golf game, but he will shoot only two or three rounds of trap and in preparation for the bird season. Go figure.

Having said much good about the clay target games, I will also note there is much that is not-so-good. First, and self evident, clay targets are not birds, and they do not fly like birds.

A clay target is traveling at its maximum speed at the moment it leaves the launcher, and it slows at a calculable rate through the rest of its flight. Typically, an upland game bird takes wing at a slow speed and increases its velocity through the course of its flight.

Allowing for some vagaries due to wind, the flight trajectory of a clay target is consistent. Clay targets do not, of their own volition, weave and dodge or change speed and direction. Wild upland birds frequently (and willfully, bless their pea-sized brains) weave and dodge and change speed and direction.

A clay target shooter knows, within certain limits, the exact moment the clay will take flight, and he knows more-or-less the direction that flight will take. The shooter may mount the gun to his shoulder before calling for the release of the target from the thrower. And he acquires, tracks, and shoots his targets on a field unobstructed by brush, trees, terrain and other impediments, or, in the case of sporting clays, he attempts to break targets that will travel through "windows" of open space where they can best be hit.

The upland bird hunter seldom if ever knows the exact moment the bird will take wing, and he is even less sure of the direction of its flight. He never has the gun mounted to shoulder when the bird flushes, and he frequently attempts shots that are obstructed by brush, trees, terrain and inclement weather. Stepping into the middle of a covey of quail, for example, can significantly affect preparation for the shot and target acquisition. It can also embarrass a skeet shooter and make him search the depths of his vocabulary for the proper words to express his discomfiture.

Upland bird hunters who want to shoot clay targets as practice for wing-shooting must beware a much worse aspect of the games. Most, if not all, are now shot for the sake of the game itself, not as practice for wing-shooting. I do not object to competitive clay target shooting and have no argument with those who love the games and shoot them year-round in tournaments and leagues. It is tremendous fun. But the demon of competitive spirit lives in all of us, and if we choose to play a game, why the object is to win it.

I caution the bird hunter to be wary of this slippery slope. Put too much focus on the game itself, and you will soon be training your body not to perform the skills of wing-shooting afield but instead the skills of shooting clay targets on the range.

This pitfall can be avoided, and here are some suggestions to help you stay out of the clutches of the demon.

First: shoot as many of the clay target games as you can. I will not attempt to list and describe the various games in this essay; doing so would require thousands of words and descriptions that are as boring as the games themselves are exciting. But you should be able to find gun clubs or ranges in your area that offer trap, skeet, trap, sporting clays, and five stand. Shoot them all so that you get the greatest possible variety of targets and target flights.

Second: although the rules of the games say you *may* mount the gun to your shoulder before calling for the release of the target, the rules do *not* say that you *must* mount the gun. I suggest that you call for the target's release and mount the gun only when the target appears. Granted you will not break as many clay targets, but you will be training your body to perform the acquire-step-swing-mount-track-shoot-follow through sequence of motion that will serve you well in shooting gamebirds afield.

Third: shoot your field gun when you shoot the games. Go to any gun club and you will see that specialized shotguns dominate the clay target sports. These guns are semi-automatics or over-unders (many trap shooters use single-barrel, break-action guns, of course), they weigh eight pounds or more, and the stocks have prominent pistol grips and raised or adjustable combs. These specialized guns may be equipped with an assortment of features to reduce recoil and muzzle jump, or to assist swing and follow through: ported muzzles, adjustable buttplate recoil pads, release triggers, forend weights, and other devices.

Matched to its specific game, this type of specialized trap gun, skeet gun, and sporting clays gun can certainly increase the number of clay targets the shooter will break. And for the clay target games, the ultimate goal is the number on the scorecard, not the form and fluidity of the shooter – the art of the sport, if you will.

The shotgun you will not see on the clay target range is the one I consider the ultimate for upland bird hunting: the classic side-by-side with straight stock and splinter forend, double triggers, fixed chokes, in 16 or 20 or 28 gauge, weighing less than seven pounds. When I shoot the clays courses with these guns, will I shoot my highest possible scores? Almost certainly not. My scores will be higher if I shoot my semi-auto sporting clays gun or my over-under skeet gun. (Yes, I have one of each. Satan persuaded me to buy them, and I am sure I will have to do centuries of purgatory time as penance for the sin of covetousness.)

But I would rather break twenty-two skeet targets shooting my 28 gauge double gun than break twenty-five shooting the semi-auto. Most days. As I mentioned, we all have our own level of pride.

Regardless of your specific quirks and passions as a shotgunner, you would be wise to shoot the clay target games as often as your time and budget allow. Next fall, in the thick of an aspen woods, a ruffed grouse will flush from an unexpected place, fly in an unexpected direction, weave around a pair of spruce trees, and fall stone dead at the report of a snapshot that you are amazed to discover that your fired yourself, automatically, artfully, smoothly. And a little voice in the back of your head will whisper, "Wobble skeet, low house six."

Do not say it aloud. Let your hunting buddies proclaim you a natural.

25

My dog clipping is, admittedly, a bit uneven. Perhaps ragged. Okay – scruffy. When I plied my trimming skills on six generations of English springers, my younger daughter used to call the look "Punker Spaniel."

Punker Spaniels

EACH MAY AND SEPTEMBER the spaniels are sheared. Their coats, which have become long and shaggy over the previous months, are magnets for every burdock and beggar's tick on the farm, and the daily brushing and combing gets to be a nuisance for me and an irritation to them.

So I attach a one-inch spacer to the blades of the Wahl pet trimmer, order the dogs to jump onto the table in the workshop, and the fall (or spring) grooming sessions get under way.

To use the word "grooming" to describe my technique in dog hair clipping is probably too complimentary. With the same deft touch that I employ with a scrub brush to scour gummy cow manure or raccoon carrion from their coats, I mow with abandon while the dogs squirm and twist.

The result is a haircut that is utilitarian, but not what you would call elegant. The goal is low maintenance, not high glamour.

My dog clipping is, admittedly, a bit uneven. Perhaps ragged. Okay – scruffy. When I plied my trimming skills on six generations of English springers, my younger daughter used to call the look "Punker Spaniel."

Hey, these are hunting dogs. Working dogs for the field. Not prissy house dogs mincing through the ring at the Westminster Kennel Club Show. My signature coiffure: picture a border collie on a six-day bender that asked for a haircut at a tattoo parlor. That's the look I strive for. Or the look I get, anyway.

Once the hour of clipping and trimming misery is over and done, the dogs are happy and I'm happy. So what's the issue?

My current *Sturm und Drang* pair of French spaniels, Sasha and Abbey, grudgingly submits to the barbering, but both communicate clearly with body language and facial expression that they are much put-upon, and this whole grooming business is annoying in the extreme. Of the two, Sasha has more reason to mope.

Although they are the same breed, their coats could not be more dissimilar. Come the first frost of fall, Sasha grows a winter pelt that would rival the woolliest Cheviot sheep from the highlands of Scotland. Beneath a top layer of long coarse outer hair lies a thick mat of fur that one would expect on this French-Canadian dog, bred to endure the bitter winters of Quebec. Hunting on a zero degree day, she frequently stretches out full-length, belly-down in a powdery snow drift to cool off, steam rising from her body.

Abbey grows a long stringy outer coat, but her under plumage is a silky layer of hair that would be the envy of an Afghan hound. She rolls in manure with enthusiasm equal to Sasha's, but she is usually easier to clean and brush afterward. More fine boned and slender than Sasha, Abbey has gone through a couple of the North Country's coldest winters in her first two years and never shown a sign of discomfort until night temperatures drop below -20 degrees and I insist on a last piddle-walk in the yard before we settle down for the night near the woodstove.

So Sasha's time on the grooming table is three times as long as Abbey's, and the pull and tug of the clipper much more forceful. Still, she complains less, probably because she has gone through this agony twenty times and accepts its inevitability.

Abbey, on the other hand, wriggles and snaps her head around, increasing the number of scoops and gouges in her coat as the clipper tilts and plunges. Even with all the wrestling, the only part of her that looks really, really bad after the trim (in my opinion) is her tail, which has its beautiful fan of feathering chopped and shaved into something that resembles the hide of a starving street dog in Bangladesh with a bad case of mange.

But it grows back in a couple months.

The spring clipping has a secondary benefit. Swept up from the workshop floor the hair fills a five gallon plastic bucket, just the right amount to make a ring around the smaller of the two gardens. I cannot guarantee that this repels rabbits and woodchucks as the organic gardening books promise, but it seems to work – in combination with the plastic owl on the fence post, the whirligigs on sticks, the aluminum strips dangling and dancing on strings, and the companion plantings of forbs that are supposed to deter the vegetable eating vermin.

It should. The way Sasha's wet fur smells after a long winter would drive me away from a grilled T-bone steak, let alone a couple dozen bitter starts of lettuce, carrots and broccoli.

But my hunting shirts probably end the season with the same range of exotic odors. Except for the distinctive aroma of cow manure.

I don't roll in that.

At least not very often.

26

The bottom line is that the advantages of overloaded rounds are largely illusory. In practical fact, the bloody things aren't worth either the expense or the discomfort. And they are discomfortable in the extreme.

So what good are 30 percent more pellets if they're giving you less effective patterns, less efficient shooting, and beating the hell out of you to boot?

- from the essay Cartridges: When Less is More, *published in the book* Shotguns and Shooting *by Michael McIntosh, (1944-2010)*

The Charge of the Light Brigade

I CALL IT "The Charge of the Light Brigade," this shotshell load I take into battle against the troops of the "Heavy Field Artillery Regiment."

    16 gauge Fiocchi hull
    Fiocchi 616 primer
    18.2 grains of Hodgdon's Universal powder
    Ballistics Products 16 gauge sporting/field wad
    1 ounce No. 7½ shot

First order of business: Although this load patterns wonderfully in my Lefever Nitro Special, I do not assume any responsibility for its performance in any other 16 gauge shotgun. But if you load a few dozen hulls and test them on a pattern board or sheet, I predict you will be pleased with the result.

Muzzle velocity averages about 1,110 feet per second, according to tests with my shooting chrony. From both barrels, one choked improved-cylinder and the other light-modified, the patterns at thirty yards are uniform, even, and consistent.

Dozens of sessions of pattern testing with all gauges of shotguns have convinced me that good patterns are almost always associated with these light loads. A loyal member of the Light Brigade, I am an outspoken advocate of light loads. As a result, I am constantly at war with Heavy Artillery boys.

In these shotgun ballistics battles, both sides are armed with a few facts and a huge arsenal of opinions. Neither side has gained a foot of ground in the thirty-plus years I have been engaged in the wars, and I doubt there will be much change in the next thirty.

So, let me stake out my position here and now: Heavy Artillery advocates, you are wrong.

Yes, I know you have all the ammunition manufacturers on your side, but this backing is financially driven. Heavy loads are expensive and manufacturers make a lot of money selling them; light loads are relatively inexpensive and not nearly so profitable, so manufacturers produce almost no good-quality light loads.

Consequently, if you are going to shoot light loads, you must take up handloading. This works well for me, because reloading is enjoyable and produces shotshells tailored specifically for my guns. A less important benefit is that the cost of a box of reloaded shotshells is about two-thirds the price of even the cheapest (and worst quality) factory ammunition. This does not mean that you will save money, however. If you have $1,000 in the annual household budget for shooting, you are still going to spend the full $1,000, factory loads or reloads, but you are going to shoot a lot more rounds if you reload.

Cost aside, there is a fundamental reason I shoot light loads: I shoot light guns. Shooting a round of skeet with light loads in a 6 1/2 pound double gun is a pleasant experience. Shooting skeet with heavy loads in that light gun is punishment. Venturing afield with a heavy gun and heavy loads, unless you are six-foot-six and 250 pounds and in excellent physical condition, is also a good way to turn an enjoyable day of recreation into a miserable endurance test.

What's my definition of light load? It is really the standard load that was determined more than a century ago to be the best charge for each shotgun gauge: 28 gauge, 3/4 ounce; 20 gauge, 7/8 ounce; 16

gauge, 1 ounce; 12 gauge, 1 1/8 ounce. If you push 12 gauge to 1 1/4 ounce of shot, you will still be within the range of its "best" load; because of its bigger bore, it has a bit more flexibility.

But the Heavy Artillery boys love firepower and believe they can extend the killing range of their guns by shooting shotshells that exceed these "best" loads by 10, 20 or even 30 percent. Waterfowl hunters may have a valid argument for increased loads, especially in steel shot, but they are shooting 12 gauge guns with oversize bores and lengthened chambers that are really 10 gauge guns. And a gun that weighs 8 1/2 or 9 pounds is not a burden in a duck blind where you are sitting all morning, not walking.

Using those heavy artillery loads in a field gun to hunt upland birds is ludicrous. Everyone is free to choose their own poison, I suppose, but what is the point of shooting 1 ounce loads in a 28 gauge gun or 1 1/4 ounce loads in a 20 gauge? The birds are frail creatures, and almost all are shot at distances less than twenty-five yards.

Ah, but heavy loads throw more lethal patterns, right? No, the Heavy Artillery Regiment is wrong about that, too.

If they would do some patterning, they would see their folly. Shotguns pattern wonderfully with the shot charges that are best for them, especially if the load is low velocity. If a heavier and higher velocity load is used, patterns become ragged and full of gaps. But few Heavy Artillery disciples shoot their heavy loads at patterning sheets, and with good reason.

To produce accurate results, a pattern test requires at least five shots on the patterning papers, and ten is even better. To assure consistent point of impact on the target, these shots must be fired from the bench, off sandbags. Even with light loads this is akin to being hit in the face by five to ten left jabs thrown by a pretty good welterweight boxer (something I remember with displeasure from my college boxing days). Pattern test heavy loads and you have chosen to take several straight rights from Evander Holyfield.

Years ago, I foolishly tried to pattern some factory-loaded 12 gauge 1 1/2 ounce, 3-inch magnum, steel shot, waterfowl loads. After three shots I had entered an ethereal plane where colors were vivid, corporeal objects became viscous, and I imagined I was having a metaphysical discussion with the Bodhisattva about spiritual peace and harmony.

That was the day I permanently enlisted in The Light Brigade.

If you want to ride with the Brigade this fall but are ambivalent about entering the world of handloading, I make this recommendation. Do your upland hunting this year with trap loads, Winchester AA or Federal Gold Medal or Remington STS. Do not buy cheap target loads; they are almost certainly loaded with soft lead shot and low quality wads, a recipe for poor patterns.

Buy standard velocity loads, not the high velocity stuff named handicap, nitro, international, or sporting clays. Choose No. 7 ½ shot size, the largest size available in trap loads. I do not recommend No. 7 ½ shot for pheasants, except the first weekend of the season when the birds are young and ignorant and most shots will be close. But I have used No. 7 ½ trap loads season-long for prairie grouse, Hungarian partridge, ruffed grouse, quail, and woodcock, and if I shot well, the load performed well.

I am confident you will be pleased with the results of this experiment and may want to go to the next step – handloading shotshells and experimenting with various loads to find those best suited to your gun.

Another benefit of light loads: the birds you shoot will not be mangled beyond recognition. Although, thinking about it, maybe that is what the Heavy Artillery boys want – birds that are, like the Wicked Witch of the East, "not just merely dead but really most sincerely dead," and easily found amid a pile of blood and feathers.

Those of us in The Light Brigade don't need to do that. We invariably have bird dogs that are good retrievers. Touché, Artillerists.

27

If there's bird hunting in heaven –
Grouse, woodcock, quail, pheasant, Huns –
Son, you can take this as Gospel:
God blesses sixteen gauge double guns.
Don't offer me some over/under,
Semi-autos and pumps don't abide,
Keep your twelve and twenty gauges;
I'll shoot a sixteen bore side-by-side.
            - Clement Seagrave

Graceful double guns

NO GENTLEMAN would hunt upland game birds with anything other than a double gun.

I will reluctantly accept an over-and-under double barrel in the field, but be aware that when I say 'double gun' I am referring to a side-by-side double barrel.

If you choose to shoot waterfowl, turkeys, or clay targets with a semi-automatic or a pump shotgun, you won't get any complaint from me. That is certainly appropriate. For one thing, if a pump gun falls out of the boat and is lost in the muck at the bottom of the marsh or lake it is no great loss. And you will almost certainly record better scores with a semi-auto than a double gun when you shoot trap, skeet, sporting clays, five-stand, and other clay target games – which are great fun but have nothing in common with upland bird hunting.

However, do not enter a northern Minnesota aspen and alder forest carrying a semi-auto and tell me it is an upland bird gun. There is a fashion of late to manufacture semi-autos that weigh six and one-half pounds with handsome checkering on the stock and some dubious quality 'engraving' on the receiver, and proclaim them bird guns. Wash an ape, comb an ape, still an ape. Paint a machine, polish a machine, still a machine.

A graceful double gun is the creation of an artist and an artisan, a thing of beauty to complement what has become a spiritual time in my life – a day afield with game birds, bird dogs and good friends. Note the word 'graceful.' This does not apply to the many blunderbuss double guns produced by American arms manufacturers for a half century.

What is a graceful double gun? Granting some 'eye of the beholder' subjectivity and bowing to the reality that stock measurements and other niceties of fit and balance depend on the physique and age and physical condition of the shooter, I will offer my definition. A graceful double gun has these characteristics:

    Weight between six and seven pounds
    Point of balance midway between the lead hand and grip hand
    Straight stock (or Prince of Wales grip)
    Stock with the least practical drop at comb and at heel
    Barrels no shorter than 28 inches and no longer than 32 inches
    Two triggers
    Solid rib
    Nicely grained walnut stock and forearm
    Splinter forend
    Well executed but not 'showy' checkering

These are more-or-less in order of priority – or at least my priorities.

Characteristics that are less important include those which can be easily modified (length of pull, choke construction, trigger pull weights, single brass front bead, tasteful recoil pad or butt plate), and those which cannot be changed but are not crucial (gauge, action type – box lock or side lock, extractors vs. ejectors). Features that eliminate a gun from consideration, for me but perhaps not for you, include ventilated rib, beavertail forend, elaborate engraving, and short barrels.

Lest you think that such a gun would be beyond your price range, I have acquired used guns that were 'close to perfect' knowing I could alter stocks, chokes, trigger pulls, butt pads, and other features until they met my criteria for graceful double gun – for considerably less than the cost of those semi-automatic machines masquerading as upland bird guns.

Some concessions and confessions are in order. I own and enjoy shooting semi-automatic and pump-action shotguns, but not for upland bird hunting. All but one of my double guns lack two or three of the 'graceful gun' criteria I have listed.

Alas, I do not shoot that 'perfect' gun as well as I shoot its 'imperfect' cousin. Both are Spanish made 28 gauges, but the ugly cousin has a single trigger, a Prince of Wales grip, a semi-beavertail forend, and a stock that is too thick at the comb. Nonetheless, it breaks an occasional twenty-five at skeet and hits most shots at woodcock and ruffed grouse, so I have learned to love its imperfections.

In the shotgun shooting game, I'm not exactly perfect myself.

28

In the presence of the storm, thunderbolts, hurricane, rain, darkness, and the lions, which might be concealed but a few paces away, he felt disarmed and helpless.
  - *from* In Desert and Wilderness, *by Henryk Sienkiewicz (1846-1916)*

Unlike the majority of people, he did not hate or fear the wilderness; as harsh as the empty lands were, they possessed a grace and a beauty that no artifice could compete with and that he found restorative.
  - *from* Inheritance, *by Christopher Paolini (born 1983)*

Red in tooth and claw

THE WILD is not a gentle place.

Our country's shrinking wilderness and those rough places I call "the wild" are endangered by those who want to tame or exploit it, but a bigger threat may be those who want to romanticize it. Neither the developers nor the romantics, I fear, have much experience in the wild. The huge majority of people, residents of urban and suburban communities, have only fleeting moments of actual contact with the wilderness, and most of their ventures are vicarious, sitting in front of a television screen.

Watching a video of a thunderstorm roaring across a woodland or prairie is nothing like huddling under a tarp in the dubious shelter of a hillside while bolts of lightning and pelting rain rage all around you. Regardless of the videographer's commitment and skill in capturing and presenting the reality of that storm in the wild, his effort will fail. All television programs that attempt to depict the reality of the outdoors are predestined to fail because we watch them in the controlled environment and comfort of the indoors, the antithesis of the wild.

We observe, as through a window, the tropical jungle's stagnant darkness dappled with dim pools of light filtered green by canopies of foliage. But we do not sweat, we do not smell the fecundity of the rotting vegetation, we do not feel the humid heaviness of the rain forest enveloping us. There are no swarms of gnats and mosquitoes gnawing on our skin and boring into our eyes, ears, noses and other tender areas. There is no pungent, musky odor rising from the paw prints of a hunting jaguar that overlay the hoof marks of the deer it is stalking.

We witness, through this insulating window, the Arctic storm forming over the sea of pack ice, the swirls of snow falling, the thick hair of the sled dogs tousled by the wind, the look of stoic resignation on the face of the Inuit guide. But we do not shiver with bitter cold, we do not feel the sting of steel-hard sleet hitting our face, we do not feel the vertiginous shift of the ice beneath our boots. There is no scent of sea salt, no icy stab in our nose and throat with each breath we take. There is no glare of harsh Arctic sunlight slashing our eyes and blinding our vision.

We are not isolated or vulnerable. We are observers, not participants. We are not walking that slippery ridgeback trail of the wild that winds its narrow way between life and death (sometimes, though rarely, our own life and death).

You can experience more "wild" in an hour sitting quiet and still in a Midwest farm's woodlot than in a week of watching video productions about the world's great remaining wilderness areas. But few people do.

A day in the wild is so foreign to city dwellers. Accustomed to recreational activities and pastimes that are fast-paced and provide immediate reward, they are literally in a foreign country when they walk off the beaten path to sample the wilderness. The spectacle of a college football game is noisily and violently thrust upon your senses; the panorama of life in a forest has to be sought out and perceived through quiet observation.

The latter experience is more rewarding to me, but clearly I am a miniscule minority compared to the tens of thousands of people in my part of the country who cram themselves into sports stadiums on an autumn afternoon. Roman emperors knew they could remain in control if they provided citizens with *panem et circenses* – bread and circuses. Burgers and football games fit the bill for the oligarchs of our civilization.

It works, even for the wilderness romantics in the population. Especially for the romantics. I have learned that many people who express their love of the wilderness actually dread and dislike it. Their fear is not of being devoured by a bear but of being nibbled to death by bugs. Well, I detest black gnats as much as the next person, but I can slap on some insect repellant. Game day traffic jams with cars full of inebriated fans swarming around me – DEET does not keep them away.

So I find myself watching the struggle between the ravagers and the revisionists: those who want to destroy the wilderness to exploit its natural resources for their financial gain versus those who want to nurture some civilized version of the wilderness to exploit its mystical image for their aesthetic pleasure. I can't abide the plunderers and can't relate to the preservationists. Neither side seems to have a true understanding – or at least my understanding – of the nature and the beauty and the value of the wild.

The best I can do is guard the small slice of the wild on my farm. And enjoy the quiet spectacle of it as often as possible.

29

A skunked dog bath recipe that really works:
  Two pints of 3 percent hydrogen peroxide
  One-fourth cup of baking soda
  One tablespoon of liquid dish washing detergent
  One pair of sturdy rubber gloves
  One gallon of water
Directions: put on the rubber gloves and mix together in the plastic bucket the hydrogen peroxide, baking soda, and dish detergent. Using this foamy solution, lather the dog from nose to tail with a liberal and energetic washing. Let stand for five or six minutes, then rinse the dog with the gallon of water.

North country skunks

SASHA loves to catch skunks.

All of my bird dogs have caught at least one skunk. For most of them, one was enough. More than enough.

Susie, Molly, Herco, Jessie, Annie – they all tangled with a single skunk and decided it was a pleasure they could forego. Pete, an English springer spaniel of great hunting and retrieving ability but no mental giant, caught and killed three of them before his dim bulb of a brain established the cause-and-effect connection between the scent of skunk in the wild and the resultant three days of swollen-eyed blindness, vomiting, and discharge of gallons of dog-snot from nose and mouth.

Sasha, a French spaniel whose versatile breed background must include a generous helping of genes from fur-hunting dogs, loves the pursuit of skunks and has caught four so far.

She has somehow avoided the super-saturation spraying that can be a life-changing experience for a bird dog and a powerful motivation to avoid certain unacceptable chase-and-catch behaviors, sort of a condensed twelve-step program with chemical enhancement.

The moderate doses of skunk spray that Sasha has received to date seem to annoy her for less than an hour, and the lingering odor she regards as an *eau de chien du chasseur* that is the envy of her kennel companions. She is indifferent to restorative measures; I would not say she enjoys a skunk scent-killer bath on a cold fall afternoon, but she does not seem to mind it that much either.

Twice, her point-leap-grab skunk catching technique has gotten me sprayed worse than her, which she may regard as a pretty good joke. To quote a wildlife department web page of information on the common striped skunk (*Mephitis mephitis*):

"A direct hit in the face causes painful but temporary blindness and severe inflammation of the eyes, nose, and mouth. Choking, coughing, some degree of nausea, and possible fainting also may result."

Yes, indeed.

My latest Sasha-induced skunking resulted in the disposal of a fairly new pair of brush-front pants, a tattered and holed shooting vest, good leather gloves, and a battered pair of hunting boots that probably needed replaced anyway. I was encouraged to sleep in a separate room, in an old sleeping bag, for several nights. For the next two years I could locate my 16 gauge double gun and my whistle lanyard in a dark room by scent alone, and to this day no one ever asks to borrow my orange crusher hunting hat.

On two occasions traumatic misadventures held promise of ending Sasha's fur-hunting desires. Years ago, on a late summer evening walk, she dropped into the slouching point that tells me she is on fur instead of feathers, but when she broke point and began barking the object of her attention proved to be a badger rather than a skunk.

A merry time ensued as Sasha chased the badger for a while and I chased Sasha. Then the badger turned and chased me as Sasha tagged along nipping and dancing. This angered the badger, which changed tactics and chased Sasha with great snarling and teeth-snapping. I grabbed a stick, ran down the badger (badgers are not especially fast runners, I learned, but they have great stamina and are aggressively persistent), and gave it a solid whack to discourage it from biting my dog. That worked well, as the badger immediately ceased trying to bite Sasha and put all its energy and focus into its attempts to bite me.

Eventually, this cops-and-robbers comedy routine reached the badger's residence at the edge of the woods, and after throwing himself around on the ground like a three-year-old child having a temper tantrum, he retreated into his den and begged me and/or Sasha to reach in and try to grab him. We declined the invitation. I mistakenly believed this harrowing experience would break Sasha of hunting fur, but in retrospect I realized she had had a wonderfully exciting time and was thus encouraged to engage in future flying-fur escapades.

That ill-directed enthusiasm led to her tussle last fall with a porcupine in the Nemadji State Forest near Duluth, Minnesota. It was a grim afternoon for her as I used a pliers to pull a couple dozen quills from her face, mouth, tongue and forelegs. Broken-off quill tips, some as long as two inches, worked their way out through her hide over the next two months.

I hope she has learned a lesson. Perhaps the scent of "fur" will now set off alarm whistles and red lights in her head, and she will back away from all encounters with porcupines, badgers, raccoons, and – most importantly – skunks. But I am not optimistic.

Consequently, I keep a three-gallon plastic bucket of skunk-bath ingredients in the box of my pickup. This recipe, taken from a web site of the North American Versatile Hunting Dog Association (NAVHDA), really works, and I offer it here for those unfortunate bird hunters whose dogs have an affinity for skunks.

Two pints of 3 percent hydrogen peroxide
One-fourth cup of baking soda
One tablespoon of liquid dish washing detergent
One pair of sturdy rubber gloves
One gallon of water

Directions: put on the rubber gloves and mix together in the plastic bucket the hydrogen peroxide, baking soda, and dish detergent. Using this foamy solution, lather the dog from nose to tail with a liberal and energetic washing. Let stand for five or six minutes, then rinse the dog with the gallon of water.

Note: Go to the store immediately after the end of the day's hunt and buy two batches-worth of these ingredients. One batch will be used to wash the dog a second time a day or two after the skunking. The other batch goes into the plastic bucket in your truck.

Because if you do not have the kit handy your dog will know it and will catch another skunk at the first opportunity. Trust me; I have learned from experience.

30

Handy as a pocket on a shirt.
- Traditional Folk Saying

Six-pocket pants

"WHY DO YOU always wear six-pocket pants?"

We members of the Over the Hill Gang, all debonair and sophisticated gentlemen, hear that question frequently. It's true, although we occasionally wear jeans or Dockers, our regular attire is six-pocket pants, and tyro bird hunters eager to emulate the old masters of the game ask us "Why?"

Our standard, if flippant, answer is: "Because we cannot find seven-pocket pants." But there are practical reasons.

Appearance is not really a consideration. All the Over The Hill Gang look good in six-pocket pants, of course, but fashion has little to do with our choice since we look suave and stylish in any attire, with the possible exception of those ridiculous three-quarter length basketball shorts that are the rage now. Admittedly, color coordination is not one of our strengths, so it helps that six-pocket pants come in earth tones – khaki, tan, gray and occasionally camo patterns – that blend with most of the shirts in our wardrobes and complement all our hunter-orange clothing.

That is all beside the point. Our preference for six-pocket pants, also known as cargo pants, is purely functional. It's the pockets.

You have heard the traditional folk saying "Handy as a pocket on a shirt." In truth, shirt pockets are far surpassed in utilitarian value by pants pockets – especially if there are several pockets and they are generously large.

With enough searching through online catalogs I suppose we could find those expensive "safari" shirts with four or even five pockets, but all shirt pockets have shortcomings. For one thing, shirt pockets are small, rarely more than half the size of a good, roomy pants pocket. And being located high on the body, shirt pockets full of heavy items tend to raise one's center of gravity, upsetting your balance and causing embarrassing tumbles in the field when crossing creeks or clambering over slippery rocks or slogging through greasy mud.

Pants pockets, in contrast, lower your center of gravity as weight is added, much like ballast in a sailing ship. With all my daily equipment distributed into the various pockets of my cargo pants, with care taken to place the heaviest items in the leg-side pockets, I am all but impossible to knock over, sort of like those round-bottomed inflatable toys that can be tipped but never toppled.

Shirt pockets can also be difficult to reach when you are in a hurry to get at some immediately needed item. However, if you have my build – the short-legged and forward-hunched endomorphic body type which one of my daughters derogatorily but affectionately refers to as "Neanderthal" – you will find the side-leg pockets of cargo pants easily accessible, literally right there at your fingertips.

Be advised, too, that your shooting proficiency can be impaired by a shirt pocket. Gear stashed in a shirt's right breast pocket (left, if you are a southpaw shooter) will interfere with your gun mount, causing you to shoot erratically. If you are given to fits of temper after a shirt-snagged, two-barrel miss on an easy shot at a towering pheasant, you will have the added problem of reallocating your gear in the field after you have ripped the offending pocket off the front of your shirt. Not that I have ever done this myself, you understand.

Most troublesome is the tendency of shirt pockets to spill at inopportune times. Shirt pockets have a way of disgorging their contents whenever you lean, bend, twist, slip or trip, and should you actually fall and/or roll you can expect all your paraphernalia in every shirt pocket will be scattered over a twenty square foot area, usually in dense foliage or under water.

These misfortunes seldom happen when wearing cargo pants with large, deep, pleated pockets with Velcro-fastened flaps. Put your spare compass in your cargo pants pocket and you will never experience that disconcerting feeling of being in unfamiliar country on a cloudy evening and not knowing the direction to the truck.

In addition to the spare compass, what does the OTH Gang pack in their pants? Let me rephrase: what items does the OTH Gang have in the pockets of their pants? Here are some of the typical things:

Pocket knife, Leatherman tool, keys, cell phone, wallet, hunting license wallet (it is best to have a separate wallet for your hunting licenses; topic for a future essay), sunglasses, handkerchief, camera, money clip, extra hearing aid batteries, spare dog whistle, pen (leak proof), notepad, wire cutters, band-aids, a couple handkerchiefs.

Carry the rest of your essential gear in the pockets and pouches of your bird hunter's strap vest: a dozen shotshells, gloves, stocking cap, rain poncho, toilet paper, water bottle, granola bar, map, butane lighter, and a topo map of the area. Add a third compass, one of those pin-on globe types that you can attach to the shoulder strap.

Dale, a charter member of the OTH Gang, tells me that I carry too much gear, but I hold to the Boy Scout motto, "Be Prepared," and my addendum, "If the thing you need is not in your pocket you might as well not own it." Besides, he has his own idiosyncrasy for overloading, namely carrying thirty or more shotshells. Opportunities to shoot a limit of birds are rare these days, but even if he had the chance to bag three woodcock and five grouse, shooting thirty rounds would be unlikely. But according to him, "You can never carry too much ammunition unless you fall into deep water or catch on fire."

So all the OTH Gang have our sound reasons for wearing six-pocket pants.

But we do get weary of being asked about it. Last October while we were eating a pre-hunt breakfast at Ernie's Diner, one of the nosey locals walked over to our table and asked, "Do you guys always wear cargo pants when you're bird hunting?"

"We didn't used to," said Ron, "But back when we hunted in our underwear our legs got chaffed by the brush and our butts got cold on windy days."

Ron was just putting him on though. We have never gone bird hunting in our underwear. At least I haven't.

31

Plink- vt. (plink; rhymes with sink) [slang, American]: to shoot informal targets such as tin cans with a small caliber rifle or handgun; the word 'plink' is an onomatopoeia of the sharp, metallic sound of a small caliber bullet hitting a tin can; n. the act or practice of plinking
        -*Definition from* North Country Dictionary *(unpublished)*
"*DO NOT PLINK.*"
        – *Jeff Cooper (1920-2006), firearms instructor, creator of the 'modern technique' of handgun shooting, and a small arms expert*
"*Plink as often as you can.*"
        - *Clement Seagrave, dedicated plinker, indifferent handgun marksman, and an expert at finding ejected brass cases*

Plinking

THERE MAY BE some grandfather-grandson pastime that is more fun and instructive than plinking, but I doubt it.

There comes a time in the grandfather-grandson relationship when plinking is the ultimate sharing and bonding activity. Plinking brings out the adult in a ten-year-old and the child in a sixty-year-old. It is the outdoor sports skill that every grandson loves to learn and every grandfather loves to teach.

Attempts by grandfathers to instruct their grandsons in the fundamentals of other sports can be risky. Calling up memories of former prowess on the baseball diamond or the football field, Grandpa is likely to overrate his diminished physical abilities. And deceived by the child's relatively small size, Grandpa is also likely to underestimate his grandson's quickness, strength and competitive nature.

When you reach a certain age, playing pitch-and-catch is going to be perilous, and the nurses at the emergency room are not likely to be sympathetic when you tell them you were fooled by the curve ball. They know ten-year-old boys don't throw the curve ball, and you were just too slow and uncoordinated to catch the fastball.

Tennis? Soccer? Volleyball? Touch football? Check your insurance policy first. And have your cell phone handy with 9-1-1 on speed-dial in readiness for that moment when your grandson asks, "Are you okay, Grandpa?" Despite your advanced years, the manly answer is, "I'm fine. Just help me up." But the orthopedic surgeon will have a different opinion.

You are wise to seek out an activity that you will both enjoy but is less physically demanding and presents no chance of injury. Computer games are out. They are an insult to someone with five decades of built-up animosity toward electronic-digital technology, and anyway I'm not engaging in any indoor activities with grandsons. They get enough of that stuff in the city. When we're together on the farm, goldarn it, we are going to get wet, cold and muddy (or hot, sweaty and dusty, depending on the weather).

Badminton, croquet, bocce, lawn skittles? Please – we're talking man sports here. If we don't have to don ball caps, camo shirts and safety glasses to play, it's not a guy thing.

Fortunately, plinking is exciting, fun and fascinating for both grandfather and grandson, and it meets all the "grandpa safety" criteria. When grandchildren come to visit the farm, I want them to have experiences that will teach them something about the outdoors – the natural world. I also want them to learn respect for the natural world and the responsibilities that go with ventures into that world.

I have three grandsons. As soon as they were big enough to safely handle a bolt-action .22 caliber rifle, I introduced them to plinking. They loved it from the first "plink." What kid could not love sitting on the deck of the garage, rifle propped on knees or sandbags, aiming at silhouette targets twenty-five yards down range, gently pulling the trigger, hearing the shot and the "plink" of the bullet, and watching the target go tumbling in the sand pit. They even accept, with manners and grace, the close supervision and coaching of grumpy Grandpa.

To be sure, we have a great advantage living in a rural area that offers both a place to safely shoot a .22 rifle and a community that still respects the sports of shooting and hunting and the people who practice them. I fear those blessings are fast-disappearing in most places. A guardian of my dying culture and ethos, I believe this loss is unfortunate because these activities teach children responsible and respectful behavior and self-confidence.

I also want my grandchildren to have hands-on experience with firearms. The way in which the use of firearms is portrayed on television programs and in motion pictures – and in the hideous video games that advocate gun violence – could be dismissed as ridiculous comedy except for the fact that it promotes careless, negligent and dangerous handling of firearms. As part of plinking, my grandchildren learn to unfailingly practice the basic firearm safety precautions:

Treat every gun as though it were loaded.

Always keep the gun muzzle pointed in a safe direction.

When you accept a firearm from someone, or hand a firearm to someone, the action must be open.

Know how the firearm operates.

Shoot on a range that is safe and has a backstop.

No firearm is to be left unattended, ever.

Children may handle a firearm only under adult supervision.

Obey the instructions of the range master (Grandpa).

They learn all this in the course of a single afternoon of plinking. The rules are reinforced each session.

There are many shooting instructors, the late Jeff Cooper included, who advise against plinking because as a training practice it can induce all sorts of bad habits: jerking the trigger, rushing the shot, canting the gun, improper sight alignment, sloppy gun mount... Yes, it is more conducive to good shooting technique to meticulously punch holes in a paper target with precise, well-disciplined rifle firing, but it is not much fun for a ten-year old. Frankly, it's not much fun for Grandpa, either.

Seeing the steel targets tumble is exciting and rewarding, and that's what you want to provide in those first shooting experiences with grandkids. If one of them starts to show the talent and desire to shoot small-bore competition someday, we'll get more serious. Until then, we're shooting for the joy of it, not for scores.

I'll end with a piece of practical advice and a confession.

The practical advice: to make some good, long-lasting targets for plinking, get some 2 ½ or 3-inch diameter steel pipe, spray paint it orange, and cut it into 4-inch lengths.

The confession: everything I've said about grandsons applies to granddaughters as well, but so far neither of my granddaughters has shown interest in plinking. I'm going to keep encouraging them.

32

If a bird fall, it is like being able to bring back a token from a dream.
    - Vance Bourjaily (1922-2010), from his book The Unnatural Enemy

If a bird fall

ALL BIRD HUNTING is creative fiction.

Perhaps it seems that way only to me, as a writer whose avocation is hunting upland birds. (Some would suggest that I am actually an upland bird hunter whose avocation is writing.)

But for every bird hunter, writer or no, when the afternoon afield is ended, the dog is back in the travel box, the shotgun in the case, the birds in the cooler, and the vest and chaps in a heap in the back of the pickup truck, the hunt goes through a metamorphosis from enactment to history to story.

If some dispassionate observer had followed this hunter unseen through the day, keeping a minute-by-minute log of events and actions, and if those factual records were compared to the fireside tales the hunter will tell come evening, mellowed and enhanced by ale or Scotch, the hunter's account would probably bear only a passing resemblance to the observer's notations.

Compare the stories told by the two or three other hunters in the day's party, and quite likely there would be few points of agreement and much dispute of the facts in their various narratives.

We compose the saga of the hunt as we go through the day, mentally recording moments and impressions and emotions, calling them up for edit and rewrite as the hunt progresses and its theme takes shape, polishing them to fit the plot, reshaping the action sequences to match the development of the adventure story we want this to be. We do these revisions at each juncture – each memorable event of the day – and then carefully save the improved version in a memory file so it can be retrieved and embellished into an even more exciting and fulfilling tale come nightfall.

We all know bird hunters who have achieved renown not so much from their expertise and prowess in the field as from their epic story-telling in camp.

Most hunters do this, at least I contend that I do this, not to grasp the laurel of fleeting fame but to satisfy a longing and a passion for the time spent hunting to be an adventure full of excitement and joy and wonder. We want to compile a storehouse of uplifting memories, recollections of bright and shining moments, that we can call up to brighten other parts of our lives that can unfortunately be numbingly dull and dispiriting. Our hunting stories evoke much-needed interludes of happiness.

You lift your spirits with that memory of the day your best-ever dog (gone now these five or ten or fifteen years) swept across the wide, shallow saddle between two ridges of low hills in the heart of the Fort Pierre National Grassland, snapped into a marble-statue point, held rigid and trembling as you jogged across two hundred yards of shortgrass prairie to her side, flushed a pod of fourteen prairie chickens, dropped two stone dead with a classic right-left double, and watched the rest fly to the far horizon as their tuk-tuk-tuk alarm calls grew fainter and their beat-beat-beat-glide winged forms became dots in a pale blue Western sky. And of course your dog made two soft-mouthed retrieves to hand.

At least that's how you remember it and how you will tell it to your dying day. And why not? It's your life story, your epic poem; surely you should have the satisfaction of being the heroic figure in a few of the chapters and verses.

In the depths of winter we take those euphoric memories out of the file in times of emotional need and inhale them furtively, like those stout cigars we are no longer supposed to enjoy. Accompanied by the scent of a wet dog at your feet, the walnut-and-steel heft of a freshly oiled double gun in your hands, and the iridescence of a tuft feathers floating out from your bird vest's game pocket, they can be arranged into a series of chapters that comprise a novel about bird seasons past, the bond between hunter and dog, the camaraderie of long-time hunting companions, the magic and mystery of the game birds, and the wonder of the primal country that is the fantastic landscape for it all.

These are life chapters unencumbered by the shadows of doubt, anxiety, fear, regret, uncertainty and failure that beset us through too many of our days. Like all familiar stories that are more fantasy than fact, we go back to them, time after time, to remind us of the true joys and passions in our lives.

So forgive me if I begin to craft the storyline of this season's bird hunts from the first moment I step into the aspen and alder woods, the shortgrass prairie, the cattail marsh, the CRP field, or the brushy waterway. I may be premature in constructing the day's tale this early on, but I do not think so. I'm yearning for the journey and the narrative to go forward in harmony, page-by-page, so I can be central to the story of discovery of the promising bird covert, the dog enticed by the first trace of scent, the anticipation that she will cautiously but surely work her way to its source. I want to turn the page to see her lock on point, tensely waiting for me to flush the crouching bird into a clattering explosion of flight. Then the shot, the fall to earth, the dog's frantic search for the dead bird, the fetch and retrieve, and the sweet anticlimax of holding this beautiful grouse or pheasant or woodcock in hand.

The writer Vance Bourjaily said it best: "If a bird fall, it is like being able to bring back a token from a dream." The bird is the proof of the success of the day's hunt, but it is also the symbol of the drama, both a flesh-and-blood animal from a wild landscape and a mythical creature from a fantasy, a token that you were at the heart of an adventure story that I fear only a dwindling few bird hunters can now read and understand.

Turn your memories into stories; it is the only way to hold onto them and share them.

33

Every man learns the trade of fatherhood through a series of on-the-job-training blunders and successes, and he has few resources to draw on beyond his memory of how his own father raised him. Given the difficulty of the task and the vagaries of chance and circumstance in life, it is no wonder that some men do exceptionally well in the father business and some are abject failures. Most of us fall somewhere between those two extremes.

Fathers and sons

IT WAS THE MOST amazing feat of rifle shooting I ever witnessed.

Eleven years of age, sitting in a southern Ohio woods on an October morning, shivering with cold in the hazy light of dawn, I first heard two squirrels doing their mating chase and then saw them running acrobatic laps around the bole of a hickory tree, about thirty yards away, four feet above the ground, sending bits of bark flying on each gravity defying circuit of the rough trunk. My father had also seen them and brought his .22 rifle to his shoulder when the squirrels were on the opposite side of the tree where they could not see his movement.

On their next lap he shot the trailing squirrel on the run, through the head, stone dead, and it dropped to the base of the tree. Less than three seconds later, the lead squirrel came around the tree again, also running at full speed and unaware that her pursuer had been dispatched. My father shot that one, too, through the head, and it dropped on top of the first squirrel lying below.

Two shots. Open sights. Thirty yards. At speeding targets the size of golf balls. Using an old Remington 550 semi-automatic, which I learned many years later was not the most accurate rifle of its era.

Two thoughts filled my head: first – my father was the greatest rifle shooter in the world; second – I would grow up and someday assume his place as the greatest rifle shooter in the world. The first of those childhood fantasies may have been true. The second was never a remote possibility; I became a mediocre shot with a rifle at best.

Since that time I have seen hunting companions make some impressive shots on running deer and antelope on Western prairies with a .243 Winchester sporting rifle, assassinations of prairie dogs at 400 yards distance with a varmint rifle in .204 Ruger caliber, and even a crow brought down on the wing with a bullet from a .22 single-shot rifle. Extraordinary shooting, but I felt there was as much luck as skill involved in those shots, and I could, perhaps with a few misses along the way, match them. I have never thought for a moment I could duplicate the back-to-back shots my father made on those squirrels.

If a final boost was needed to lift my father onto the lofty pedestal of hero worship that morning of squirrel hunting was it. All fathers are heroes to their sons. At least until we go through that painful time in our lives when we discover that they are men, not demigods, and they have feet of clay, just like us. Then we feel somehow betrayed by our naïveté and the blindness of our worship, and it may be many years before we can rebuild a loving relationship, this time a friendship between grown men rather than the intrinsic and instinctive bond between father and son.

During that most impressionable period of our boyhood years, say between the ages of six and fourteen, we create what proves to be an unsteady foundation for that later relationship because there is often much unrealistic expectation, both from the child-man-son toward his father and from the man-child-father toward his son. Every man learns the trade of fatherhood through a series of on-the-job-training blunders and successes, and he has few resources to draw on beyond his memory of how his own father raised him. Given the difficulty of the task and the vagaries of chance and circumstance in life, it is no wonder that some men do exceptionally well in the father business and some are abject failures. Most of us fall somewhere between those two extremes.

A close friend of mine once confided that he felt his father "pretty much lost interest" in him during his early teenage years when it became apparent he would not become a star baseball player or a world class mechanical engineer. The irony is that he did become a world class mechanical engineer and industrial design innovator. But he, like most of us, will live out his life with a shadowed corner of his psyche reminding him that he does not, nor will he ever, live up to his father's expectations.

Frustrated with my obsession with project details and quality and deadlines, my wife once pleaded with me, "Why don't you just quit for the night and start again tomorrow?" to which I blurted out, "Because Dad wouldn't like it!" A shadowed corner of my own psyche. Perhaps we all live in that shadow.

My father's ghostly monitoring of my life has lightened somewhat over the years as my appreciation of him has grown. I look at the few photographs taken of him in his youth, especially those of his time in the Army in World War II, pictures of a skinny nineteen-year-old in the midst of another 200 skinny, shiny-faced boys in poorly fitting uniforms, smiling and eager to do their part in a world at war, blissfully unaware of the horrors they would meet.

I have become more understanding of what I once perceived as his shortcomings and more admiring of his strengths and accomplishments. A child of the Great Depression who was drafted into military service while still in high school, he fought and survived D-Day on the beaches of Normandy, the hedgerow war across France, the Battle of the Bulge, the offense against Germany's Siegfried Line, and the final months of the infantryman's war until Germany's surrender.

He came home to finish his education, marry, raise a family, hold down a weekday job and do contract work of his own on weekends for more than thirty years until a series of heart ailments and surgeries ended his working days. He was surely one of those men the journalist Tom Brokaw calls "The Greatest Generation." Would I have done as well? I wonder.

I respect the character and the fortitude of the men and women of the Greatest Generation, but I know from first-hand experience that most folks of that generation carried a lot of baggage that was not so great: blatant racial and national prejudice, gender bias, intolerance of people and ideas outside the conventional, disdain for knowledge beyond their realm, unquestioning acceptance of the status quo. Late in my father's life and midway through mine, we found some common ground and could chain the guard dogs of our respective presumptions and passions. Through it all we could share hunting.

A faded black-and-white photograph of my father hangs in my "clubhouse," the room where all my outdoor gear and memories are stored away. Clad in blotchy camouflage jacket and pants, face streaked with lines of camo paint, he stands beside a whitetail buck hanging from the rafters of my garage in a small town in northeast Nebraska – the first deer he took with a bow – bursting with pride but too reserved to show it, except for the light beaming from his eyes.

He was fifty-two, more than ten years younger than I am now. I remember feeling that Nebraska deer was a gift of sorts from me to him, a payback for all he had done to make me the man I became.

The photograph was packed away in a box somewhere for years and years. When he died two years ago it came to light while going through his things. On my wall near his photo hangs his old Herter's brand compound bow. In my gun safe is his Marlin 39 lever-action .22, a rifle he had wanted all his life and that my two brothers and I gave him as a Christmas present when he was forty-five. He shot that rifle ever better than he did the Remington 550 that he used to make the two most incredible shots in the history of squirrel hunting. I could never come close to matching his rifle shooting skill, but I was probably a better wing shooter; that was a bit of an annoyance for him, I think, so we were even.

At the end of our years together, his pedestal of honor was not so tall that we could not see eye-to-eye, but he was still up there.

Damn, I was lucky to have a father like that.

34

"Boy," he said, "I will tell you a very wise thing. If a man is really intelligent, there's practically nothing a good dog can't teach him."
    –from his essay Old Dogs and Old Men Smell Bad, *from the book* The Old Man and the Boy, *by Robert Ruark (1915-65)*

Gus the enforcer

IF GUS SAYS "Down!" your belly better hit the ground in less than two seconds or you are going to be knocked rolling.

Gus is a seventy-five pound German shepherd. He does not tolerate misbehavior in my French spaniels. They are Francaise. He is Teutonic. They are canine revelers. He is a police dog.

When *les petite mademoiselles* Abbey and Sasha bounce out of their kennel runs for the morning walk on the farm, *der oberst hauptmann* Gus stands waiting. Each of the boisterous ladies runs a circle around him. He barks twice. They stop and drop. He tilts his head and utters his guttural yowl. They dash across the yard to the weedy edge of the dry run, squat, and piddle. He sniffs his approval and points to the lane leading up to the hayfield. They dash away.

Gus turns and looks back at me. "*Kommen sie, schnell!*" he orders. I *kommen. Schnell.*

Before Gus took command, the morning walks were not so orderly or well-mannered. Abbey has always been full of piss and vinegar, and every day for two years she has harassed and tormented Sasha. She likes to irritate me, too, always dancing on the edge of obedience, not blatantly ignoring my commands but obeying them lackadaisically in her own sweet time.

"Stop!" I would shout at Abbey as she bumped and pushed Sasha, pulled her ears, head-butted her, and did a little jab-and-dodge taunting. After two or three "Stops!" Abbey would cease and desist until she thought I was no longer watching. Then she'd be back at it.

If I tried physical punishment, she would cry and squeal and passively threaten to file a complaint with the ASPCA, but it did not change her attitude one whit.

I had no idea how to correct her behavior. Gus did.

About a month ago, Gus joined our dog pack while his owners, our daughter and her family, are moving from Japan to Nebraska. Despite his size, Gus is a lap dog, a teddy bear, but a dedicated family dog. A rescue dog with a bit of collie mixed with his shepherd genes, Gus is constantly herding, guarding and worrying about us.

Gus also worries about our duo of French spaniels. He worries that they are simpletons and clowns, the ne'er-d-wells of the canine world. He sized them up when he first met them, and he immediately pegged them as fools – bird hunting *idiot savants* with no other useful skills or purpose in life. And no appreciation for discipline or proper behavior. In short, French.

Gus showed no animosity toward them, only condescension. They romped around him, licked his face, sniffed his rear, rubbed against him, stretched out on their bellies, barked. He looked at me askance. "You approve of these antics?" he seemed to ask.

He tolerated them, and me, for three days. Then he took charge.

I know nothing about the characteristic behavioral traits and personality of the German shepherd breeds. Sure, I have raised and trained more than a dozen dogs, but they have all been bird dogs. The hunting came naturally, all of them eagerly learned a dozen commands, and most of them have had a loosey-goosey, happy-go-lucky attitude about life. Between hunting seasons, we pal around together on the farm, drink beer, talk about hunts past and future, and sometimes sleep together in a pile on the couch in my clubhouse. Bird dogs, in my experience, are up for anything you want to do, especially if it involves a little craziness.

German shepherds? No. That is not what they are about.

Gus wants discipline and order. Firm discipline. Precise order. Always.

Once Gus understood that I disapproved of Abbey's manic morning behavior, he took corrective action. When Abbey blasted out of her kennel door and began to badger Sasha, Gus imposed himself between them and barked once. Even I, who speak no German at all, recognized the bark as *"Nicht mehr!"* Abbey did not nicht. Instead she gave Gus a playful push with her front paws and said, *"Mon chérie*, I am the princess here, and I do as I please."

Thump-a-tumble-thud!

Gus stood stiff-legged over Abbey's prostrate body as her head slowly cleared from the spinning caused by a high, hard tackle followed by a double somersault under a seventy-five pound rolling pin. *"Sheissvogel!"* said Gus. "Your princess days are over. Now you do as I say."

He let Abbey up, and she gave a good shake to remove the dirt and grass from her coat. She put her nose in the air, and looked to me for support. "You deserved it," I told her.

As we walked up the lane to the hayfield Abbey regained her debutante attitude and bounded toward Sasha, ready to jump on her and wrestle.

"Nicht," said Gus.

"Hey, I'm not bothering you," sassed Abbey, "so you don't tell me what…"

Thump-a-tumble-thud! Bird dog down. No discussion, no warning, no exceptions, no remorse. You will obey orders, Gus's body language clearly said, or you will go rolling.

And that was that. Abbey, and Sasha for that matter, has sworn off any behavior that resembles harassment, torment, sparring, teasing or horseplay. Gus makes the rules, and they play by the rules.

This was a great achievement, and I have expressed to Gus my gratitude and admiration for his excellent training work. It is a technique I cannot exactly duplicate since I doubt, given my age and infirmities, that I could run Abbey down, tackle her, roll her over a few times, and pin her to the ground under me. But it did teach me that one must take immediate and direct action and be unfailingly consistent in applying correction if you have a dog that challenges your authority, regardless of how sweet and affectionate the dog may be.

With a few more weeks of work, Gus had Abbey squared away on a whole range of issues. It will be interesting to see if she does any backsliding when he leaves the farm for his home in Omaha. I have already cautioned Abbey: "I know where Gus will be living, and I can bring him back to the farm anytime you get too big for your britches."

All well and good, but last Saturday the story of Gus took a new twist. I had mowed for about three hours on a hot day, a chore Gus seems to love. He follows behind me and inspects the quality of my work, I suspect, as the DR Mower drags me up and down the grassy hillside. We sat in the shade that afternoon and shared a bottle of water during a fifteen-minute break. When I got to my feet, still overheated and panting, Gus moved between me and the mower.

"Time to do the rest of the hill," I told him as I patted his head and reached for the ignition key.

"*Nicht!*" said Gus.

I *nicht-ed*. Plenty of time to mow after I put him back into his kennel run, I reasoned. No use risking a roll down the hillside with a German shepherd on a hot day.

Addendum. Gus is named for Argos the faithful dog of Odysseus in Homer's epic poem *The Odyssey*. Renown in his prime for his strength, speed and tracking ability, Argos had become ill and feeble from the ravages of age and neglect during the twenty years that Odysseus wandered and struggled to return from the war in Troy to his home country of Ithaca. Of all Odyesseus's subjects when he ruled as king, only Argos recognized him when he entered his home disguised as a beggar. Argos had only strength enough to perk his ears and wag his tail as Odysseus walked by, and then lay down and died, his life fulfilled now that his master had returned at last.

Gus the Enforcer has many noble and endearing traits, but great hunting ability and steadfast loyalty do not appear to be among them. As far as I am concerned, his skills as a peacemaker and arbiter of his peers' behavior are far more valuable qualities.

35

We get too soon old and too late smart.
– Appalachian folk saying

Random advice

FOLLOWING THE EXAMPLE of Benjamin Franklin in America's colonial era when he published snippets of wit and wisdom in his annual *Poor Richard's Almanac*, I have decided to share some bits of common sense and practical advice that I have accumulated over the decades.

Franklin's collection of folk sayings, adages, and truisms has been called "sage counsel with a dash of cynicism." Mine may be better described as "bitter vetch with a dollop of skepticism." Ben was a young and optimistic Poor Richard whose advice is based on the theme "I want to tell you..." I am an old and pessimistic Curmudgeon whose advice is based on the theme "I told you so..."

Ben said "Early to bed and early to rise makes a man healthy, wealthy and wise." I say: "Early to bed and early to rise and your girl goes out with other guys."

The following aphorisms, axioms and observations are all original and completely mine. Except for the ones I stole from someone else. Or overheard in a coffee shop or bar. Or read somewhere. Or saw spray painted on the side of a building or train car. In short, most of them are borderline plagiarism, and the rest are outright plagiarism. But they are all in the public domain now, and I'm not giving anyone else rightful credit for any of them.

So, here are sixty-five wisdoms, in no particular order, that I have acquired through trial and error over the past sixty-five years. Profit from this compilation of hard-earned lessons as you will.

Look up at the stars every chance you get.

It may be better to be a live jackal than a dead lion, but it is even better to be a live lion.

If all you have is a hammer, everything looks like a nail.

Every forest has its grizzly bear.

A one-eyed man is a prophet in the land of the blind.

If the pitcher fools you with a curve ball, and you have less than two strikes, do not swing.

Rap is not music.

Helping people is the purpose of your life.

Contentment is not having what you want but wanting what you have.

An educated ape is still an ape.

When you attempt a double on game birds on the wing, shoot the trailing bird first.

The fats, sugars, starches, and oils in donuts may shorten your life. So what? Life is short anyway. Eat all the donuts you can.

Bats are Satan's flying rats from hell.

If you are hunting doves, you cannot carry too much ammunition unless you expect to fall into deep water or catch on fire.

A dog is not man's best friend. A dog is a bad friend, but an incredibly loyal and hard working pack member – if you are the pack leader.

Get it in writing.

There ain't no such thing as a free lunch.

A corporation has only one purpose: to make money for its investors.

The most adamant Christians are not.

If momma ain't happy, ain't nobody gonna be happy.

Pay cash.

Tip generously.

Hunting rifles are offered in more than 100 different calibers; the only ones you really need are a .30-06 and a .22 long rifle.

If you are a hunter, buy a pickup truck; all the messy, dirty, and smelly stuff can go in the box.

Bargains aren't.

Go fishing only in good weather.

Coffee is the true miracle drug.

Drink good beers.

Spend time with people who make you happy.

Fight only as a last resort.

If you have to fight, fight to win.

Mow the lawn in the cool of the evening.

Gardening is the most beneficial thing you will do in your life.

Plant trees.

Do not make important decisions when you are tired, hungry, angry, or confused.

We all wear uniforms.

Every medication has at least one side effect.

Do the work you like the most, not the work that pays the most.

Physical beauty is not a virtue.

Make a good plan, but remember that chance and circumstance will make you change it day-to-day.

Most of the great things in life happen at the wrong time, and the rest don't happen at all.

Time spent with a friend is always fleeting.

Write every day if you want to be a good writer.

Dream big and pursue your dreams, but set realistic goals.

Take your time and do it right the first time.

There are some things in life you must never, never, never surrender until death.

Courage is not fearlessness. Courage is overcoming fear to do the right thing.

You will learn more from failure than from success.

Sing. Yes, you can.

Someday, perhaps in your lifetime, the wild lands and the wilderness will be gone. Get out into it now, whenever you can.

Learn that all life comes from the sun, water, soil, and air.

Speak truth to power.

All actions have unexpected results.

Tell her you love her. Tell him you love him.

When your children are young, hold them every chance you get.

Time does not heal all wounds; some hurts never end.

We are all in this boat together, so everybody has to row, and everybody gets to share the beer.

Solitude regenerates your soul.

Be gracious in defeat. Be even more gracious in victory.

It is better to give than to receive, especially in boxing.

Your children will learn more from what you do than from what you say.

Convince your boss it was his idea.

Don't sweat the small stuff.

If you plan to go through life as a one-trick pony, it better be a really good trick.

Try to hit the ball as hard as you can, every damned time.

36

Shooting afield without the aid of a trained dog is very poor sport indeed... ...for it is not only the large number of birds brought to bag that inspires and gratifies, but rather it is the fine performance of his faithful dog that leads to the highest appreciation and enjoyment of the sport.
    -from the book The Amateur Trainer, *first edition published 1893, by Ed F. Haberlein*

Bird dog art

IT WAS LOVE at first sight.

My love affair with bird dogs began in my childhood when I first saw those romantic illustrations of pointers, setters, spaniels and retrievers that were featured on the posters and calendars published by ammunition manufacturers. Most memorable are the wonderful hunting scenes commissioned by the Winchester, Western, Remington, UMC, and Peters companies.

Spellbound and mesmerized by those idyllic images, I became an acolyte of the credo of bird hunting and a devotee of gun dogs of all breeds. To this day I remain a sucker for gun dog art.

We bird hunters of a certain age are intimately familiar with those illustrations and prints that were popular from the late 19th century through the 1950s, images of elegant hunting dogs in action that seemed to appear everywhere in that sportsmen's world to which we so fervently aspired – the trap range clubhouse, hardware store, service station, the musty farmers exchange office, even the walls of the milk house or tool shed. We studied them, memorized them, and projected ourselves into them.

There we were, afield with a pair of picture perfect setters, classic double gun in hand, unflustered by the rise of the covey of quail, ready to take a right-left double and then release the dogs from point to make the retrieves. Until the reverie was shattered by an uncle shouting, "Will you hurry up with that damned pitchfork and throw the manure out of these stalls?!"

Hunting dog art also adorned shotshell boxes, postcards, and the covers of *Field & Stream* and *Outdoor Life* magazines. They fired my imagination, caught me by the heartstrings, and never let go. I desperately wanted one of those dogs. My mind burned to own, train and go afield with a graceful, steadfast bird dog before me. Pheasants, grouse, quail, woodcock, ducks – all would fall to the unerring nose of my canine partner and the renowned accuracy of my shooting.

The artistic style of those illustrations was far different from the intricately detailed realism practiced by more contemporary wildlife artists and print makers. Those older depictions of outdoor sport more closely resemble the works of neo-impressionist painters or perhaps the romantic artists of the Hudson River School of landscape painting. That is as it should be; memories of bird hunting are more romance than realism.

Over the past few years there has been a revival of works from the bygone era of bird dog art, or at least a surge in interest in re-creations of hunting illustrations from a past that we remember as more slow-paced, more pleasurable, and certainly more hopeful. The most frequently encountered example of this revival is the "historic" wall calendar. The days and dates for 1902 and 2014 correspond, for example, so there is a memorabilia market for newly printed copies of century-old calendars decorated with hunting scenes that must have quickened the pulse of Teddy Roosevelt.

Fifty years of shooting over bird dogs, many of them extraordinarily good bird dogs, has made me aware that the grace and style of the dog afield does not often match the fanciful image of those flawless setters and pointers from the golden ages of hunting portraits. But sometimes reality meets and even exceeds the beauty and wonder of art, and those are the days that come flashing back, memories as clear and clean and crisp as an October morning, when we glimpse one of the romantic paintings of gun dogs in action.

I want to put on vest and hat, take a double gun in hand, step into the scene, and go walking off toward that promising covert in the company of beautiful dogs and a boon hunting companion.

Art as life, life as art.

37

...the street of the city (of heaven) was pure gold...
– Revelations 21:21

Heaven's roads are gravel and sand

WHEN THE APOSTLE JOHN wrote the Book of Revelations at age 92, a prisoner of Rome on the island of Patmos, his vision of heaven was said to have been divinely inspired. Maybe so, but I think he was mistaken about the streets being made of gold.

The streets of heaven are country roads of gravel and sand.

Everyone is entitled to his own vision of heaven. Let me tell you mine.

Heaven is a country with air so clean it almost hurts to take a deep breath in the pale light at sunrise. Every morning is early fall – except for occasional days of Indian summer – and when you awake you have that "opening day of bird season" feeling of excitement and anticipation. You walk out onto the dew-wetted deck with a cup of coffee in hand and listen to the quiet. Heaven is peacefully quiet, a place far away from the automobile, the telephone, the radio, the computer.

There are rolling hills in my part of heaven, broken by woods, hay fields, and quite a few sections of weedy cropland. Crisp-leaved autumn corn and heavy headed wheat are trimmed with icy-white frost in morning, and the cattle crowded in the tree-sheltered corner of your pasture steam in the cool air with that heavy sweet smell. The oaks in the woodlot hold onto the last of their brown-gold leaves, and the limbs of the walnut and maple trees are already winter-black and bare.

Wander down into the woods and lean again a rough tree trunk, still and silent, and you will hear the rustle and chatter of squirrels caching their winter store of acorns and walnuts. An indistinct murmuring sound, like the faraway laughter of children, makes you look up through the branches to see a straggling V of geese or a gaggle of sandhill cranes flying south, a mile high.

Heaven is a small house almost invisible in a cluster of trees at the base of a hill. It's more of a cabin, really, with a big stone chimney and a steeply peaked roof over the upstairs bedroom loft. Outside is a huge stack of firewood to feed the Franklin stove in the parlor and the cook stove in the kitchen.

On the east side are the high-fenced kennel runs, and when the cabin's front door creaks open a tall graceful setter, a bouncing springer spaniel, and a square-headed Chesapeake Bay retriever all look up in anticipation. They see you are wearing your shooting coat and boots and carrying a gun in the crook of your elbow. What will it be today, they wonder?

Heaven is strictly for trim and beautiful double guns, by the way, automatics and pumps being the inventions of the devil.

About an hour's walk north brings you to a fresh water marsh, formed by a fast flowing creek that spreads out into a dozen finger rivulets through the flood plain of a slow-moving river. A broken down duck blind on the bank is covered with brittle cattails many years old, and inside is a mesh bag of decoys that need to be set out just-so in the backwater slough where the mallards like to come after their morning feed in the cornfields. The decoys need painting, badly. But no matter: the ducks here always swarm into the blocks, even if the noise you make with a pin oak call is not the best rendition of the "kank-kank-kank" greeting call.

You won't shoot waterfowl any better in heaven than you do in your mortal life, but your Chessie will never fail to make a retrieve, or hard-mouth a bird. At least mine doesn't.

Go east from the cabin a few miles and you will find a flatter country with thick aspen stands, cut by broad draws. This used to be hard scrabble farm land, but it has been abandoned and taken over by clumps of birch, aspen, wild plum, and service berry, and thickets of wild raspberry, gooseberry, and stunted cedars. At the bottoms of the draws you'll slog from island to island through mushy bogs ringed by alders and small oaks. Take the setter on this trip. Bell him, because he'll work almost silently across the soft ground. When the bell stops, he'll be locked on point over a ground-hugging woodcock in the thickets over a pair of ruffed grouse under a tangle of wild plum.

Sadly, you will still miss a lot of shots in the aspens, even here in heaven, and some days the soupy black water of the bogs will still be just an inch or two higher than the tops of your boots. But on the walk home you can always wander through the old orchard to find a few apples, wrinkly and cider sweet, that have escaped the first frosts.

Head south the next morning into the country of grain fields and weedy ditches for a day of pheasant and quail hunting. If there is a more exciting minute in the bird hunting field than watching a hyperactive spring spaniel work a rooster pheasant out of a brush pile at the end of a drainage ditch, well I haven't experienced it. The bird finally has to explode out of the cover into the bright sunlight in a burst of green and red and gold, the gun comes up without your even thinking about it, and the springer races out into the corn stubble to bring this trophy rooster to hand, its tail feathers three feet long, or so it seems.

As you place the bird gently in the game pouch of your vest, you see the setter on point over a covey of quail a hundred yards away. Springers always "hup" and "heel" immediately on command in heaven, and they never bust a covey in front of a pointing dog, so you can take your time walking over there and enjoy the beauty of your setter's picture perfect point. Remember to reload the gun before you flush the birds.

A longer journey west from the cabin will take you into open range, the shortgrass prairie and the sandhills. This no-trees country is full or birds – sharptail grouse, prairie chickens, and a few coveys of gray partridge on the edges of wheat fields. Let the setter run big and keep the springer and the Chessie in close. Walk with the wind – trust me on this; that's the way to hunt these birds – and as you top each rise or ridge your heart will be in your throat with the expectation that a pod of a dozen grouse or chickens will burst out of the wild-rose-studded grass or a sandy hillside blowout where they have been dusting, making that raucous "tuk-tuk-tuk-tuk-tuk" alarm call and looking too squat and blunt to fly far. But they do. Very far.

You'll know where to find some stock ponds, none bigger than an acre or two, covered with ducks. Short-leash the Chessie to your belt as you crawl over the dam, and make him lie flat on his belly while you jump to you feet and holler, "Hey, ducks!" They will go up all in a cloud with a roar of wings that sounds like canvas ripping, and that big open Western sky will be full of flash and color. If you can stay calm and pick out just one or two to shoot, your dog will be swimming back with bird in mouth before the flock high overhead has made its second wide circle around you, looking for a safer, hidden pond.

There will be plenty of unexpected encounters in heaven, too. The day your springer flushes a covey of chukars, the morning those big black-footed Canada geese drop right down on top of your blind, the long-bearded turkey that goes thundering out of the woodlot corner from under your setter's nose. Almost every time afield you'll see whitetail deer, mule deer, pronghorns, coyotes, maybe even a timber wolf or a black bear. The woods are full of squirrels, cottontails, fox, raccoons, woodchucks, badgers, and a hundred species of songbirds and raptors. But there are no grizzlies, and if heaven doesn't have any skunks I'd be okay with that.

At twilight, come home to the warm house and the smell of baking bread. Bring the dogs into the mud room to clean them up, and then let them lie in front of the wood stove to get warm and dry before you feed them and put them up for the night.

As you walk them out to their kennels, look up into the ink-black sky and gaze at the stars, each one clear and big and bright. Pull your jacket close about you so you can stand silently in the cold and watch the moon rise, listening to the yip and howl of coyotes as they start their nighttime hunt.

A dinner of roast pheasant, wrapped in strips of bacon, with the summer's last cucumbers and onions, is followed by a mug of ale and maybe a cigar. Before you drop off to sleep under a too-warm down comforter you savor the scents of the cabin: wood smoke, fresh split pine and elm, coffee, soap, waxed cloth, oiled leather, gun solvent and oil, still a trace of wet dog.

That's my vision of heaven. No streets of gold for me. I'll walk those country roads of gravel and sand.

38

When I heard those words on the telephone – "Dave's gone"- I did not feel the emptiness of death but only the loneliness of departure, as if I had been told, "Dave's left on his elk hunting trip to the mountains."

Gone on ahead

WHEN THE TELELPHONE RANG early Friday morning I looked at the numbers displayed on the caller-ID screen and knew what the message would be. I picked up the receiver and a voice at the other end said, "Dave's gone."

Dave Wade, my friend and hunting companion for almost forty years had died.

His passing was not unexpected. His body had been battered and devastated by cancer over the previous four years, and the fight against the disease had called for powerful drugs, hormones, chemicals and radiation treatments that had also damaged and debilitated him physically.

Mentally and spiritually, he never wavered. Over the final year, when he knew that treatments could not cure the cancer but only slow its inevitable progress, he accepted his fate with courage, grace, and dignity. He was, in fact, the touchstone of strength and resolve when friends and family faltered. He had no fear of death, although he was frustrated and exasperated that it was robbing him of fifteen or twenty years of time and adventures he wanted to share with his grandchildren.

Up until the final days of his life he was hosting visitors at his home, sitting on his south deck in the warm morning sunshine, looking out over the thirty acres of his land in southeast Nebraska that he had shaped and groomed as wildlife habitat. He talked with us about the state of his food plots, the burst of aquatic life the rainy summer had given his pond, the increase in the number of species of song birds on the place during the past few years. He also talked effusively about the upcoming Texas hog hunt he had arranged in August for his two sons, son-in-law, and grandson-in-law.

Dave Wade was a hunter nonpareil. Hunting was not just his avocation, it was his religion, his spiritual foundation. His hours afield with a muzzle-loader rifle or a recurve bow in his hands were not hunts so much as they were sacred ventures into that natural world of wonders and delights that he knew better than most of us know our backyards.

Along with a passion for bow hunting, he taught me the most valuable lesson about the sport: the joy is not in the taking of game but in the act of hunting itself, from the first minutes of scouting new country for sign until the last fading light of evening when you returned, exhausted but rejuvenated and contented, to camp or home. If I had learned nothing more than that our friendship would have been invaluable to me, but he taught me much more about the skills and nuances of hunting, and why it is important to know and abide by the ethic and standards of fair chase and sportsmanship.

He also taught me that a deeper satisfaction in hunting, especially as we have grown older, is making the hunt exciting and enjoyable and successful for the next generations of hunters. It is much more gratifying and rewarding to have your son-in-law shoot a nice buck the two of you have scouted than it is to shoot that buck yourself. There is a lesson not just for hunting but for life: Our purpose in this world is to help other people and make their lives better.

Dave was a member of the American Long Rifle Association, a group that is passionate (some would say fanatic) about researching, recreating, and re-enacting life in colonial America's "long hunter" era from about 1750 until 1815. The association values historic accuracy, and its members are truly reliving history at their encampments, equipped with authentic clothing, gear, rifles and tools of that period.

Dave's stories about his ALRA adventures – or misadventures – in the wild regions of the Appalachian Mountains made listeners aware that he may have been born two hundred years too late to find his perfect calling in life. I know he was tough as a pine knot and determined as a badger after a gopher when he was faced with hardships of the hunt, camp and trail. He was deadly accurate with his flintlock rifles, and handy with a tomahawk and knife. His den featured prints and artwork that depicted the era of the long hunter, and I think he secretly wished he could have lived during that time. He would have become an eighteenth century legend.

A self-made man in the tradition of American rugged individualism, Dave rose from a poor and sometimes rough childhood to become a good college football player and graduate to a career as a high school teacher, coach, principal, and superintendent. He was a mentor and motivator of dozens of students from backgrounds similar to his, encouraging, pushing and cajoling them to believe in themselves and succeed. Late in his life, many of them came calling to express their appreciation and their admiration for what he had done to shape their lives.

Dave was a friend with whom I could share all dreams, frustrations, ambitions, disappointments, triumphs, hopes and fears. We made a connection the first time we met, and although we might get together only once or twice a year, each time it was as though we had been together just the day before and we were picking up right where we left off. His passing has left a hole in my life, and perhaps in my spirit and soul, that can never be filled.

Yet, a strange but somehow comforting thought formed in my mind when I heard those words on the telephone: "Dave's gone." I did not feel the emptiness of death but only the loneliness of departure, as if I had been told, "Dave's left on his elk hunting trip to the mountains."

My heart simply does not believe he has passed away, and insists that we are going to meet up again, although I do not know where or when, and we will pick up right where we left off. Until then I have a backlog of memories and stories to sort through, reminders of the blessings of having a heart-to-heart friend and hunting companion.

Keep the fire burning and the stew pot bubbling, Dave, while I walk these last long miles back to camp.

Jerry Johnson, author, curmudgeon, bird hunter, and dog trainer, lives in the North Country of the upper Midwest. His blog, *Dispatches from a Northern Town*, features stories about bird hunting, bird dogs, and bird guns; memoirs, social and political commentary, and other pieces of creative non-fiction. He has published two novels: *Hunting Birds – The Lives and Legends of the Pine Country Rod, Gun, Dog and Social Club*, and *Scrawny Dog, Hungry Cat, and Fat Rat – A Tragedy for Children*. Both are available in paperback and Kindle editions at *amazon.com*. A former newspaper reporter, photographer, editor, columnist, and public relations director, he and his wife Patti live in a 130-year-old log house on the small farm they manage for wildlife habitat. He hunts, fishes, and shoots clay target games with a group of friends that call themselves The Over the Hill Gang.

The stories and essays published in this book are versions of pieces that were originally posted 2013-14 on the blog *Dispatches from a Northern Town – A Curmudgeon's Commentary*, by Jerry Johnson.

Made in the USA
San Bernardino, CA
16 January 2015